# Pioneers of Colonial Virginia

BEING A COLLECTION OF NARRATIVES
OF
INFLUENTIAL AND
LESS WELL-KNOWN PIONEERS
IN
COLONIAL VIRGINIA
AND
THEIR IMPACT ON SOCIETY

Volume 2

David C. Joyce

HERITAGE BOOKS
2020

# HERITAGE BOOKS
*AN IMPRINT OF HERITAGE BOOKS, INC.*

## Books, CDs, and more—Worldwide

For our listing of thousands of titles see our website
at
www.HeritageBooks.com

Published 2020 by
HERITAGE BOOKS, INC.
Publishing Division
5810 Ruatan Street
Berwyn Heights, Md. 20740

Copyright © 2020 David C. Joyce

Heritage Books by the author:

*Pioneers of Colonial Virginia: Being a Collection of Narratives of Influential and Less Well-Known Pioneers in Colonial Virginia and Their Impact on Society Volumes 1 and 2*

David Joyce is a professional genealogist specializing in eighteenth-century Virginia. The author of *Pioneers of Colonial Virginia*, he educates others on the genealogy and history of colonial Virginia. He has been published in the *Magazine of Virginia Genealogy* and *Yourgenealogytoday*. He can be reached at www.chroniclesofcolonialvirginia.com/

David Joyce would like to thank the Barrow Family Association of America for their assistance in the publication of this book.

Original cover art by Debra Joyce.

All rights reserved. No part of this book may be reproduced or transmitted in any form or by any means, electronic or mechanical, including photocopying, recording or by any information storage and retrieval system without written permission from the author, except for the inclusion of brief quotations in a review.

International Standard Book Number
Paperbound: 978-0-7884-5811-8

In honor of my aunt, Clara Rena Barrow, who inspired a love for genealogy and family

# Contents

| | |
|---|---|
| Preface and Acknowledgments | vii |
| Introduction | ix |
| Chapter 1 - Abraham Sallé | 1 |
| Chapter 2 - Alexander Joyce | 15 |
| Chapter 3 - David Barrow | 37 |
| Chapter 4 - John Dickins | 55 |
| Chapter 5 - Sarah Winston Syme Henry | 71 |
| Chapter 6 - Thomas Smith | 85 |
| Index | 103 |

# Preface and Acknowledgements

The ecclesiastical history of colonial Virginia, impacted by ongoing political and economic strife, had a profound influence on the development of the United States. Surviving religious and political persecutions imposed on them by the Church of England, religious dissenters played a significant role in shaping the history of Virginia.

These narratives, primarily based on less well-known religious leaders, highlight their efforts to reform and revitalize society. Accounts of these religious pioneers include: Abraham Sallé, Alexander Joyce, David Barrow, John Dickins, Sarah Winston Syme Henry, and Thomas Smith. Without their efforts to promote religious tolerance, establish their denominations on the frontier, and challenge the norms of their commonly-accepted culture, Virginia would have turned out very differently.

I would like to thank the Barrow Family Association of America for their assistance in the publication of this book. I also wish to thank Debra Joyce for painting the cover for this book, and Jim Joyce and Marion Wortham Joyce for their feedback concerning the chapter on Alexander Joyce. Thomas Joyce, James Webster, Virginia Turnbull, and Barbara Noe Kennedy also deserve credit for proofreading this work.

David C. Joyce
June 7, 2019

# Introduction

It is well-known that politics and religion were important factors in colonial Virginia. Determining the role of government and how it interacted with various Christian denominations, everyone was affected. From the Established Church of England's secular and ecclesiastical dominance to the resolve of religious dissenters to reform society, the history of Virginia was being built. Although most of these pioneers are now forgotten, they all played a crucial role.

In the colony of Virginia, the expansion of the frontier was clearly associated with these early settlers. Seeking new opportunities, it was not uncommon for explorers to settle on the outskirts of the then-known world. Encompassing members of the Church of England, Calvinists, Baptists, Methodists, and the Society of Friends (Quakers), they all sought improved economic prospects. In most cases, non-Anglicans also sought religious and political toleration. An excellent example of a settler seeking these freedoms is Abraham Sallé, a French Huguenot. Forced to flee France due to severe religious, political, and economic persecution, he was instrumental in establishing the Huguenot settlement of Manakin Town. A testament to the Huguenot's enduring spirit, Abraham's story provides a good example of how the frontier expanded with the assistance of religious dissenters.

Comparable to the struggles of the French Calvinists, Scots-Irish Presbyterians had a similar impact on colonial society. Fleeing political and religious persecution, their contributions to Virginia had far-reaching consequences. In their persistence to worship according to their faith, great strides were made in planting the seeds of religious freedom. Despite the restrictive rules imposed on them by the Church of England, these pioneers managed to change the history of Virginia forever. However, freedom of religion wasn't the only result of the activities of religious nonconformists.

While most dissenting Christian leaders supported the movement to abolish the restrictions placed on them, they did not challenge one of the most egregious institutions of the era: slavery.

Now considered immortal, the economic system of slavery was entrenched in colonial society. However, there was one ecclesiastical leader, the Rev. David Barrow, who attempted to abolish the slave trade. A member of the Baptist denomination, he paved the way for future emancipators. Even though his deeds now are largely forgotten, he, nevertheless, was a noteworthy pioneer. His actions inspired other like-minded Christians and left an enduring mark on Virginia society.

Among these revolutionaries was the Anglican minister, the Rev. John Dickins. A member of the Methodist movement, he was dedicated to reforming the Church of England. As Presbyterians, Baptists, and Quakers were gaining influence and growing in number, his denomination was losing members. Through his efforts to revitalize the church's message and to educate slaves, he helped preserve the Anglican faith in the colony. However, not all influential pioneers were members of the clergy

The life of Sarah Winston Syme Henry reminds us of these unsung, non-clergy pioneers. An ordinary parishioner of a Presbyterian community, the role she played inspired the birth of the United States. Even though she raised a family like other hard-working parents, her guidance helped determine the future of one of our now-famous American forefathers, Patrick Henry. The lessons she taught him about religious and civil liberties remained with Patrick even into adulthood. The consequences of this upbringing had such an impact that even the most loyal British subject was convinced by Patrick's argument to join the American cause.

The Rev. Thomas Smith, who was raised within the Anglican Church, is an example of such a person. A loyal member of his denomination, he stayed true to the Established Church's spiritual values but disagreed with it politically. At the outbreak of the American Revolution, after being forced to side with the Patriots, he would have a substantial impact on his community. Under his guidance, his Parish separated from the Church of England to affiliate themselves with the American cause.

All of these pioneers, regardless of their social status, were instrumental in the historical development of Virginia. Without their efforts to promote religious tolerance, establish their denominations on the frontier, and challenge the norms of society, the culture of Virginia would have turned out differently.

# Chapter 1
# Abraham Sallé

The foundation of the Virginia Colony, like its sister colonies, mainly consisted of immigrants. Arriving from Ireland, Scotland, Germany, and England, they played an important role in the economic and political stability in the New World. Leaving their ancestral homeland for more freedoms, they risked everything to create a new life for themselves and their families on the frontier. Some of these immigrants came to Virginia due to tragic circumstances. One such group were the French Huguenots.

The story of Abraham Sallé is an example of one of these persons. Raised in a hostile environment, he experienced severe economic and religious suppression. As a protestant in France, Abraham Sallé, a Huguenot, was threatened with imprisonment and death by the Catholic government. Forbidden from *"civil employments"* and *"from the learned professions,"*[1],[2] to having their *"goods confiscated,"*[3] the Huguenots suffered greatly. Nevertheless, the story of Abraham Sallé is not without hope. Enduring the dangerous voyage to the New World, he immigrated to Virginia and made a better life for himself and for those who followed him.

---

[1] Charles Washing Baird, *History of the Huguenot Emigration to America: Volume 1* (New York, New York : Dodd, Mead & Company, 1885), 314.
[2] Baird, *History of the Huguenot Emigration to America: Volume 1*, 314.
[3] Ibid.

**Abraham Sallé:** Born February 22, 1674, in Saint Martin, Annix, France;[4] died after March 1719 in Henrico County, Virginia.[5]

**Abraham Sallé's Parentage:** Jean Sallé and Maria Martin.[6]

**Life Story:** From his birth in 1674 on the Isle of Ré to his death in 1719 in Virginia, Abraham lived a chaotic existence. Raised in an environment where French Huguenots were legally persecuted, Abraham's childhood was one surrounded by fear and death. Although he lived in an almost constant state of fear, this also motivated him to flee France.

In the year 1674, the place of his birth was a peaceful place. Situated miles from the persecutions in the rest of France, he lived a safe life. The situation changed, however, with the appointment of Governor Demuyn, who was*"a mortal enemy of Protestantism."*[7] Once a haven for fleeing Huguenots, under Demuyn the Isle of Ré became a target of the French monarch.

Under Demuyn's administration, all aspects of society became restrictive. Forbidden to participate in the government, French Protestants could no longer work as educated professionals. Nor were they allowed to promulgate the teachings of John Calvin, the founder of the Presbyterian Church. Huguenot ministers that persisted in preaching were humiliated and imprisoned.

---

[4] Benjamin B. Weisiger, III, *Henrico County Virginia Colonial Wills & Deeds (1677-1737)*, (Athens, Georgia : Iberian Publishing Company, 1998), 201; Ancestry, *"Family Data Collection – Births,"* "database, *Ancestry.com* (http://www.ancestry.com : accessed 3 February 2018) entry for Marcus Abraham Salle, baptized 22 February 1674.

[5] Weisiger, III, *Henrico County Virginia Colonial Wills & Deeds (1677-1737)*, 201.

[6] Ancestry, *"Family Data Collection – Births,"* "database entry for Marcus Abraham Salle, baptized 22 February 1674.

[7] Charles Washing Baird, *History of the Huguenot Emigration to America: Volume 1* (New York, New York: Dodd, Mead & Company, 1885), 312.

During his youth, Abraham Sallé observed these dreadful acts inflicted upon his countrymen. From manhunts that led to victims being *"dragged out of doors,"* having their *"throat[s] cut,"*[8] to public hangings,[9] the punishments were never-ending. The French authorities even tied Protestants to horses' *"tail[s]"*,[10] and dragged them across town.

Beginning in 1685 the infamous dragonnades invaded Abraham's neighborhood and forced themselves into the resident's homes.[11] Abusing the families by pressuring them to convert to Catholicism, it was common for these soldiers to inflict upon the residence.

Seeing no alternative, Abraham fled to Protestant England. Under the cloak of darkness, he disguised himself as a *"mendicant"* and *"passed through the places where they were most exposed to suspicion."*[12] Making his way to the coast, he boarded a ship and sailed to the United Kingdom, where he was welcomed with open arms.

With previous generations of Huguenots having already established themselves in England, they became an essential part of the English economy. Known for their contributions to science, weaving, writing, and government, they became a cornerstone of English society.

Surprised at the freedoms given to the French Protestants in England, Abraham rejoiced. Given the right to practice his Presbyterian doctrines, he was granted citizenship and was able to

---

[8] 8. James Fontaine, *A Tale of the Huguenots, or Memoirs of a French Refugee Family* (London, England: Forgotten Books, 2015), 22.
[9] James Fontaine, *A Tale of the Huguenots, or Memoirs of a French Refugee Family* (London, England: Forgotten Books, 2015), 46.
[10] James Fontaine, *A Tale of the Huguenots, or Memoirs of a French Refugee Family*, 50.
[11] .ibid
[12] Charles Washing Baird, *History of the Huguenot Emigration to America: Volume 1* (New York, New York: Dodd, Mead & Company, 1885), 253.

enroll his children in English schools.[13] However, this was not the full extent of the Huguenots' welcome. Ordered to *"give them a kind reception,"* English officials were to *"furnish them [French Huguenots] with free passports, and grant them all assistance and furtherance in their journeys to the places whither they might desire to go."*[14]

Unfortunately, this good fortune was not long-lived. As time passed, French Presbyterians were pressured into adopting *"the orders of the Protestant Church of England and the Book of Common Prayers."*[15] This policy had the effect of dividing the Huguenot community. While some were satisfied with their new freedoms, others felt unduly restricted by this new policy.

In 1699, Abraham married Olive Perault in London, England.[16] They did not remain there long, however. On November 17, 1700, their firstborn son, Abraham, was baptized in New York.[17] The following year, their second son, Jacob, was baptized in the same French Church in New York.

The reason Abraham moved to the New World was the same as with other French Huguenots: he preferred to join his countrymen in the northern colonies.[18] It is unknown what prospects Abraham

---

[13] Charles Washing Baird, *History of the Huguenot Emigration to America: Volume 1* (New York, New York: Dodd, Mead & Company, 1885), 254.

[14] Charles Washing Baird, *History of the Huguenot Emigration to America: Volume 1* (New York, New York: Dodd, Mead & Company, 1885), 255

[15] Debra Guiou Stufflebean, A French Huguenot Legacy (United States: Amazon, 2011), 58; digital images, Google Books (http://www.books.google.com: accessed 6 February 2018).

[16] Edmund West, "*Family Data Collection – Marriages*," "database, *Ancestry* (http://www.ancestry.com: accessed 6 February 2018), entry for Marcus Abraham Sallee and Olive Perault; 1699.

[17] French Church du Saint Espirt, *Registers of the Births, Marriages, and Deaths of the "Eglise Françoise À la Nouvelle York."*(New York, New York: Genealogical Publishing Company, 1886), 77; digital Images, *Google Books* (http://www.books.google.com: accessed 7 February 2018).

[18] Charles Washing Baird, *History of the Huguenot Emigration to America: Volume 1* (New York, New York: Dodd, Mead & Company, 1885), 166; digital

Sallé had in New York City, but he was yet again looking for a more stable situation. However, after the birth of Jacob,[19] a new opportunity in Virginia presented itself.

In Virginia the western frontier was expanding offering William III, King of England, a promising prospect. Ordering his colonial representatives to find accommodations for a Huguenot settlement,[20] the swamps of Norfolk, Virginia, were considered. But due to *"ye air of it very moist and unhealthy,"*[21] this locality was rejected.

Finally, deciding on the *"upper part of the James River,"*[22] the government prepared for the arrival of hundreds of French immigrants. Allocating 10,000 acres of land for these refugees, King William III, gave each family 133 acres.[23] Attracted by the promise of acquiring new land, Abraham took advantage of this unique opportunity for himself and his family.

On December 20, 1707, seven years after the establishment of Manakin Town in Henrico County, Virginia, Abraham Sallé is

---

images, *Google Books* (http://www.google.books.com: accessed 7 February 2018).

[19] French Church du Saint Espirt, *Registers of the Births, Marriages, and Deaths of the "Eglise Françoise À la Nouvelle York."* (New York, New York: Genealogical Publishing Company, 1886), 77; digital Images, *Google Books* (http://www.books.google.com: accessed 7 February 2018).

[20] R. A. Brock, *Documents, Chiefly Unpublished, Relating To The Huguenot Emigration* (London, England: Forgotten Books, 2015), 5-8.

[21] R. A. Brock, *Documents, Chiefly Unpublished, Relating To The Huguenot Emigration* (London, England: Forgotten Books, 2015), 6.

[22] R. A. Brock, *Documents, Chiefly Unpublished, Relating To The Huguenot Emigration*, 6.

[23] King William Parish, The *Vestry Book of King William Parish (1707-1750)*, (Greenville, South Carolina: Southern Historic Press, Inc.,1966), 2; The Huguenot Society of the Founders of Manakin Town in the Colony of Virginia, *Original 1704 Land Grant* (http://huguenot-manakin.org/manakin/landgrant.php: accessed 7 February 2018), "*1704 Land Grant of 10,000 Acres from the Colony of Virginia to the French Huguenots.*"

recorded as a vestryman in the King William Parish.[24] Charged with the maintenance of the parish, he had to *"control and regulate the expenditure of the Parish funds,"*[25] and *"elect some of the parochial officers."*[26]

Unlike other parishes, King William Parish was given the right to govern itself.[27] This independence allowed parish members to worship as they pleased,[28] and provided them with freedoms that the majority of religious dissenters were denied.

This benefit, however, came at a cost: the Huguenots of Manakin Town were required to adopt the structure of the Church of England. In the Presbyterian denomination, it was the elders that managed the church, but now vestrymen made these decisions. This change pulled Abraham Sallé into a controversial debate.

On March 27, 1707, acting as justice of the peace, Abraham became entangled in a dispute with the minister, Mr. Philipe.[29] The incident began awkwardly but grew into a worse situation. One evening after Mr. Philipe finished the daily sermon, he demanded that the *"Register of Christenings to be delivered up to him out of ye Clerk of the Vestry."*[30] And, contrary to church doctrine, he threated to excommunicate the clerk if he refused to comply.

---

[24] King William Parish, The *Vestry Book of King William Parish (1707-1750)*, (Greenville, South Carolina: Southern Historic Press, Inc.,1966), 8.
[25] Henry Mason Baum, *The Rights and Duties of Rectors, Churchwardens and Vestryman in the American Church* (Philadelphia, Pennsylvania: Claxton, Remsen & Haffelfinger, 1879), 288; digital images, *Google Books* (http://www.books.google.com: accessed 7 February 2018).
[26] Baum, *The Rights and Duties of Rectors, Churchwardens and Vestryman in the American Church*, 288.
[27] King William Parish, The *Vestry Book of King William Parish (1707-1750)*, 2.
[28] *Ibid*
[29] King William Parish, The *Vestry Book of King William Parish (1707-1750)*, (Greenville, South Carolina: Southern Historic Press, Inc., 1966), 19-20.
[30] R. A. Brock, *Documents, Chiefly Unpublished, Relating To The Huguenot Emigration* (London, England: Forgotten Books, 2015), 69.

Determined to maintain order, Abraham assured Mr. Philipe that *"the Vestry had no intention either to encroach upon his Rights or to give up their own."*[31] He stressed that the vestrymen had to *"inform themselves"* for an appropriate resolution to the situation.[32]

Outraged, the minister lashed out, claiming there was no vestry. As a justice of the peace, Abraham knew that political strife had become problematic for the community. Representing the English Crown, he had a civic duty to perform, and an obligation to serve the Huguenot community. Before he could respond appropriately, however, Mr. Philip had incited a mob.

*"Many injurious things"* were uttered against Abraham and the crowd increased their harassment.[33] Yelling for Abraham's assassination, the justice of the peace was forced to leave the building, after which, he called Mr. Philipe *"Chief of the Seditious."*[34]

This conflict troubled Abraham deeply. With discord now in Manakin Town and his reputation tarnished, his future seemed dim. Fortunately, this did not last. On April 7, 1707, after an inspection of the church register, Abraham discovered that Mr. Philipe had tampered with the church minutes.[35] Removing all references to the dispute that occurred on March 27, 1707, Mr. Philipe also had erased all evidence against himself. Despite Mr. Philipes's attempt, however, Abraham's character remained intact.

---

[31] R. A. Brock, *Documents, Chiefly Unpublished, Relating To The Huguenot Emigration*, 69.
[32] *Ibid*
[33] *Ibid*
[34] R. A. Brock, *Documents, Chiefly Unpublished, Relating To The Huguenot Emigration*, 70.
[35] King William Parish, The *Vestry Book of King William Parish (1707-1750)*, (Greenville, South Carolina: Southern Historic Press, Inc., 1966), 20-21.

With crisis averted and order restored, Manakin Town could move forward again. Although resentment over this controversy continued to divide the French Huguenots, Abraham focused on expanding the settlement. Over time, Manakin Town became known for its *"piety, thrift, and successful industry."*[36]

In 1707, beginning with the establishment of King William Parish, Abraham helped inspire the progressive nature of Manakin Town and proved to be a successful leader.

As Manakin town grew due to an influx of new refugees, the 5,000 acres that previously were granted were now insufficient for the community's needs. Acting on behalf of the Huguenots, on November 18, 1710, Abraham petitioned the Governor's Council to give them the remaining 5,000 acres.[37]

Despite having been given plenty of land, Manakin Town's began to decline. With the Huguenots eventually marrying into other frontier families, the settlement became deserted.[38] But despite this, the church chapel remains standing today and endures as a historic landmark.

On December 31, 1715, four years before his death, Abraham was elected Clerk of King William Parish.[39] Elected by the vestry, he was responsible for recording the church minutes.[40] This job, essential to the parish, also involved dealing with financial,

---

[36] King William Parish, The *Vestry Book of King William Parish (1707-1750)*, (Greenville, South Carolina: Southern Historic Press, Inc., 1966), 3.
[37] R. A. Brock, *Documents, Chiefly Unpublished, Relating To The Huguenot Emigration* (London, England: Forgotten Books, 2015), 71-72.
[38] King William Parish, The *Vestry Book of King William Parish (1707-1750)*, (Greenville, South Carolina: Southern Historic Press, Inc.,1966), 4.
[39] King William Parish, The *Vestry Book of King William Parish (1707-1750)*, 41.
[40] Henry Mason Baum, *The Rights and Duties of Rectors, Churchwardens and Vestryman in the American Church* (Philadelphia, Pennsylvania: Claxton, Remsen & Haffelfinger, 1879), 290; digital images, *Google Books* (http://www.books.google.com: accessed 9 February 2018).

governmental, and ecclesiastical matters. When Mathieu Bonsergent, on behalf of the parish was given a *"weak child"* to *"be nourished and cared for in like manner as his own (children), well and worthily, for the space of five years,"*[41] Abraham Sallé was there to document it.

At the height of his career, Abraham was rewarded for his service. On November 25, 1718, he was granted *"six † pounds per year"* for *"performing the duties of clerk or secretary of the present vestry, and reader in the church."*[42]

## Children

The children of Abraham Sallé and Olive Perault are as follows:
- **Abraham Sallé:** Born November 17, 1700 in New York;[43] died March 1730 in Henrico County, Virginia.[44] He married Magdalen.[45]
- **Jacob Sallé**: Born 1701 in New York;[46] place and date of death unknown.
- **Isaac Sallé**: Born in Manakin Town, Virginia;[47] died 1730 in Goochland County, Virginia.[48]

---

[41] King William Parish, The *Vestry Book of King William Parish (1707-1750)*, 41.
[42] King William Parish, The *Vestry Book of King William Parish (1707-1750)*, (Greenville, South Carolina: Southern Historic Press, Inc., 1966), 45.
[43] French Church du Saint Espirt, *Registers of the Births, Marriages, and Deaths of the "Eglise Françoise À la Nouvelle York*, 77.
[44] Benjamin B. Wisiger III, *Henrico County Virginia Colonial Wills & Deeds (1677-1737)*, (Athens, Georgia: Iberian Publishing Company, 1998), 152.
[45] Wisiger, *Henrico County Virginia Colonial Wills & Deeds (1677-1737)*, 152.
[46] French Church du Saint Espirt, *Registers of the Births, Marriages, and Deaths of the "Eglise Françoise À la Nouvelle York."* (New York, New York: Genealogical Publishing Company, 1886), 83; digital Images, *Google Books* (http://www.books.google.com: accessed 9 February 2018).
[47] Benjamin B. Wisiger III, *Henrico County Virginia Colonial Wills & Deeds (1677-1737)*, (Athens, Georgia: Iberian Publishing Company, 1998), 201.

- **William Sallé**: Born in Manakin Town, Virginia;[49] died in Buckingham County, Virginia.
- **Peter (Pierre) Sallé**: Born in Manakin Town, Virginia;[50] died November 27, 1752, in Cumberland County, Virginia.[51] He married Frances Bondurant.[52]
- **Olive Magdalen Sallé**: Born in Manakin Town, Virginia;[53] place and date of death unknown. She married Etienne Malet.[54]

**Conclusion**

Born into a life-threatening environment, Abraham Sallé, a French Protestant, grew up in an atmosphere of harsh religious and political persecution. Fleeing France, he sailed for England where his kinsmen had been granted unusual liberties. These freedoms, however, came with conditions that challenged their Presbyterian doctrine. Disheartened by these circumstances, he immigrated to New York where he found great religious liberty. Several years later, Abraham moved to Manakin Town on the frontier of Virginia. Attracted by the opportunity to be a landowner and to

---

[48] William McFarlane Jones, *The Douglas Register* (1928; reprint, Baltimore : Maryland: Genealogical Publishing Company, 2001), 403.
[49] Wisiger, *Henrico County Virginia Colonial Wills & Deeds (1677-1737)*, 201.
[50] Ibid
[51] Edmund West, "*Family Data Collection –deaths*, "database, *Ancestry* (http://www.ancestry.com: accessed 9 February 2018), entry for Pierre Sallee, 27 November 1752, Cumberland County, Virginia.
[52] William McFarlane Jones, *The Douglas Register* (1928; reprint, Baltimore: Maryland: Genealogical Publishing Company, 2001), 384; John Bennett Boddie, *Historical Southern Families. Volume I* (1947; reprint, Baltimore, Maryland: Genealogical Publishing Company, 1994), 144; digital images, *Ancestry* (http://www.ancestry.com: accessed 9 February 2018).
[53] Wisiger, *Henrico County Virginia Colonial Wills & Deeds (1677-1737)*, 201; Boddie, *Historical Southern Families. Volume I*, 144.
[54] Boddie, *Historical Southern Families. Volume I*, 144.

join the growing Huguenot settlement there, he became one of its leaders. Representing both church and state, he proved to be a capable official, helping to transform the community into a prosperous colony. By the end of his life, he had helped create a new, positive identity for French Huguenots, inspiring them to look toward the future.

- Born on February 22, 1674, in Saint Martin, Annix, France;[55] he was born into an era of prejudice. Subject to political and religious persecution, his fellow Presbyterians were killed and imprisoned by King Louis XIV.
- During his childhood, he witnessed victims being *"dragged out of doors"* where their throats were cut. In other cases, protestants were tied to *"horse's tail[s]"* and paraded through town.[56]
- Disguised as a *"mendicant,"* Abraham fled France as he *"passed through the places where they were most exposed to suspicion."*[57]
- Immigrating to London, England, the English officials were ordered to *"give them a kind reception,"* and to *"furnish them with free passports, and grant them all assistance and furtherance in their journeys."*[58]

After his arrival, French Presbyterians were pressured into adopting *"the orders of the Protestant Church of England and the*

---

[55] *Henrico County Virginia Colonial Wills & Deeds (1677-1737)*, 201; Ancestry, "Family Data Collection – Births, entry for Marcus Abraham Salle, baptized 22 February 1674.
[56] Fontaine, *A Tale of the Huguenots, or Memoirs of a French Refugee Family*, 22, 46.
[57] Baird, *History of the Huguenot Emigration to America: Volume I*, 253.
[58] Baird, *History of the Huguenot Emigration to America: Volume I*, 255.

*Book of Common Prayers.*"[59] Disagreeing with this compromise, Abraham traveled to New York where he could freely worship.[60]

- Several years after his wife gave birth to his first sons, Abraham and Jacob;[61] he moved to the Huguenot settlement of Manakin Town, Virginia.
- First recorded as a vestryman in King William Parish on December 7, 1707,[62] he had become an influential leader. Tasked with making important decisions, he had to *"control and regulate the expenditure of the Parish funds,"*[63] and to *"elect some of the parochial officers."*[64]
- Acting as justice of the peace, he became involved in a dispute with Mr. Philip, the parish minister.[65] Inciting a mob against Abraham Sallé, Mr. Philip claimed that there was no vestry. Forced to leave the chapel, Abraham defended himself, calling the minister, *"Chief of the Seditious."*[66]
- As a church official, Abraham was familiar with the compromise between the English government and his kinsmen. Allowed to govern their parish, they were required to adopt the vestry model of the Church of England.[67]

---

[59] Stufflebean, A French Huguenot Legacy, 58.
[60] French Church du Saint Espirt, *Registers of the Births, Marriages, and Deaths of the "Eglise Françoise À la Nouvelle York."*,77, 83.
[61] Ibid
[62] King William Parish, The *Vestry Book of King William Parish (1707-1750),* 8.
[63] Baum, *The Rights and Duties of Rectors, Churchwardens and Vestryman in the American Church,* 288.
[64] Ibid
[65] . King William Parish, *The Vestry Book of King William Parish (1707-1750), 19-20.*
[66] R. A. Brock, *Documents, Chiefly Unpublished, Relating To The Huguenot Emigration,* 69.
[67] King William Parish, *The Vestry Book of King William Parish (1707-1750),* 2.

- On November 18, 1710, he successfully petitioned the Governor's Council of Virginia to grant an additional 5,000 acres of land to the French Huguenots.[68]
- Rewarded "*six † pounds per year*" for "*performing the duties of clerk* "on November 25, 1718,[69] Abraham had reached the height of his career. During this time, he participated in charitable events, especially when it concerned helping orphans and the needy.

---

[68] Brock, *Documents, Chiefly Unpublished, Relating To The Huguenot Emigration*, 71-72.
[69] King William Parish, *The Vestry Book of King William Parish (1707-1750)*, 45.

# Chapter 2
# Alexander Joyce

From the founding of the Virginia Colony, the exploration of the frontier was essential to its survival. Beginning with the efforts of pioneers that settled on the outskirts of civilization, the history of America was just beginning. Responsible for expanding the government further into the countryside, British officials played an important role in colonialism. However, there was another entity that exerted great influence in developing the colony: the Presbyterian Church.

Under the leadership of itinerant Presbyterian ministers and elders, new settlements were established in the backcountry. One of these leaders, Alexander Joyce, played a crucial role in settling Lunenburg County, Virginia. Although he is not mentioned in the history books of Southside Virginia, Alexander's leadership in county affairs was influential. Serving as a ruling elder, surveyor, farmer, and advocate for religious tolerance, he was instrumental in helping establish the Presbyterian community of Cub Creek.

**Alexander's parentage**: The son of Thomas Joyce, whose father was a Scottish laird, and Mary Blaikley, he grew up in County Down, Ireland.[1]

---

[1] Ros Davies, "Welcome to People's Names of Co. Down, Ireland," *Ros Davies' Co. Down, Northern Ireland Family Research Site* (http://www.rosdavies.com: accessed 26 November 2018), entry for Thomas Joyce and Mary Blaikley; citing Ballynahinch Presbyterian Church Registers.

**Alexander Joyce**: Born January 1720 in Ballynahinch, County Down, Ireland;[2] died March 3, 1778, in Guilford County, North Carolina.[3] He married Sarah Austin, probably in central Virginia. After Sarah's death, he married Jane Hamilton in Prince Edward County, Virginia, in 1758.[4]

**Life Story**: The childhood of Alexander Joyce was characterized by hardship and controversy. He and his family experienced severe economic depression, political persecution, religious persecution, and famine. Oppressed by the English government, he faced obstacles from every part of society. Whether he was being punished by English officials or scorned by his British and Irish neighbors, there seemed to be no end to Alexander's difficulties.

Before his birth in 1720, the British Government had passed an act that crippled the economy of County Down, Ireland. Redirecting the trade of wool exclusively to England and Wales, the livelihood of workers suffered.[5] With their income severely limited, most families were reduced to poverty.

With his family being unable to support itself, Alexander faced starvation. The economy in shambles, landlords *"doubled or trebled"* their rent,[6] the consequence of which made farming unprofitable. However, this wasn't the only adverse circumstance

---

[2] Ros Davies, "Welcome to People's Names of Co. Down, Ireland," *Ros Davies' Co. Down, Northern Ireland Family Research Site* (http://www.rosdavies.com: accessed 26 November 2018), entry for Alexander Joyce baptized January 1720; citing Ballynahinch Presbyterian Church Registers.

[3] "Alexander Joyce (1720-1778) 1778 Will: Part 1-2," March 1778; digital image, *Descendants of Alexander and Thomas Joyce Families Association*, Documentation (https://www.thomasandalexanderjoyceassociation.com/documentation: accessed 26 November 2018).

[4] Prince Edward County, *"Virginia, Marriage Bonds, 1754-1850,"* page number not mentioned, Alexander Joyce to Jane Hamilton; microfilm 40; Library of Virginia, Richmond, Virginia.

[5] Wayland F. Dunaway, *The Scotch-Irish of Colonial Pennsylvania* (Chapel Hill, North Carolina: The University of North Carolina Press, 1944), 29.

[6] Dunaway, *The Scotch-Irish of Colonial Pennsylvania*, 29.

affecting their food supply. *"Reoccurring bad harvests"* also made it nearly impossible to raise a family.[7]

Additionally, as a Presbyterian, Alexander suffered greatly as well. Considered religious dissenters by the Established Church of England, Presbyterians were penalized by the British government. Subject to *"unjust laws and petty persecutions,"*[8] Alexander's community was affected severely. Forced to pay unaffordable tithes to the Anglican clergy, Alexander and his family fell into debt.[9]

Denied citizenship,[10] almost every aspect of Presbyterian life was negatively impacted. The institution of marriage among Presbyterians was threatened by the Church of England officials. Declaring marriages performed by Presbyterian ministers illegal, pastors were fined and brought to court.[11] *"Excluding them [Presbyterians] from all places of public trust,"*[12] they were not permitted to hold public office.

Around 1740, by the time Alexander was in his twenties, he had survived the troubles of Northern Ireland and had grown into a strong-willed, adventurous settler. Like Thomas Joyce, his father in Ireland, who escaped famine in Banff, Scotland for a better life, Alexander now faced a similar dilemma. Soon, he too emigrated in search of better opportunities and a new life.

During the time of his emigration, County Down, Ireland, suffered one of its worst famines.[13] Known as *"Year of the Slaughter,"*[14]

---

[7] Wayland F. Dunaway, *The Scotch-Irish of Colonial Pennsylvania* (Chapel Hill, North Carolina: The University of North Carolina Press, 1944), 30.
[8] Wayland F. Dunaway, *The Scotch-Irish of Colonial Pennsylvania* (Chapel Hill, North Carolina: The University of North Carolina Press, 1944), 31.
[9] Dunaway, *The Scotch-Irish of Colonial Pennsylvania*, 31.
[10] Ibid
[11] Ibid
[12] Ibid
[13] Dunaway, *The Scotch-Irish of Colonial Pennsylvania*, 30.

County Down was *"almost emptied of their [its] protestant inhabitants."*[15] As a result, it is estimated that as many as 480,000 people died from the severely cold weather.[16] Determined to find a place of refuge for himself, Alexander left his native Ireland and set sail for a brave new world.

By this time, thousands of Scots-Irish Presbyterians had traveled across the Atlantic Ocean in search of a better life in Pennsylvania. Attracted by the promise of religious tolerance offered by William Penn,[17] they finally would find freedom in the colonies. Because of the gracious welcome they received, Scots-Irish communities multiplied in Pennsylvania. However, this welcome was not long-lived

When Alexander arrived in Pennsylvania, the situation had changed dramatically. Alarmed by the *"great numbers"* of Scots-Irish arriving every year,[18] native Pennsylvanians made adaptations to *"Deale"* with the Scots-Irish in such great numbers.[19] The impact of their arrival was so influential that *"men of stature feared that the swarms of Irish and Germans would transform the province beyond recognition and imperil their position in society."*[20]

---

[14] Jason King, *The History of the Irish Famine: Volume 3* (New York, NY: Rutledge, 2019), part 3; digital images, *Google Books* (http://www.books.Google.com : accessed 1 12 2018).
[15] Wayland F. Dunaway, *The Scotch-Irish of Colonial Pennsylvania* (Chapel Hill, North Carolina: The University of North Carolina Press, 1944), 40.
[16] Jason King, *The History of the Irish Famine: Volume 3*, part 3.
[17] Parke Rouse, Jr, *The Great Wagon Road* (Richmond, Virginia: The Dietz Press, 2016), 53.
[18] Patrick Griffin, *The People with No Name: Ireland's Ulster Scots, America's Scots-Irish, And the Creation of a British Atlantic World 1689-1764* (Princeton, New Jersey: Prince University Press, 2001), 101.
[19] Griffin, *The People with No Name: Ireland's Ulster Scots, America's Scots-Irish, And the Creation of a British Atlantic World 1689-1764*, 101.
[20] Ibid.

While little is known about Alexander's life in Pennsylvania, what is known is that he, like many Scots-Irish immigrants, had to venture farther south for new opportunities. With more-established families already living on land in the north of Pennsylvania, its southern border was unsettled. However, Alexander set forth on an even more ambitious journey: Traveling to the Virginia Colony on the Great Wagon Road, he became part of a historic migration.

Initially, a series of paths used by Native Americans,[21] the Great Wagon Road became an important route for early settlers heading south and west. Stretching from Philadelphia to North Carolina and beyond,[22] this highway became essential in the exploration and settling of the New World. Serving as a route for trade and migration, the Scots-Irish Presbyterians depended upon it for their future prospects.

After a long and tiresome journey, Alexander is recorded as settling on the frontier of Louisa County, Virginia on August 15 1748,[23] an area where established families were thriving.

As a religious dissenter, Alexander was attracted to this wilderness community where Presbyterians were residing in close-knit neighborhoods. Here he formed strong and lasting friendships with pioneers who disagreed with the Church of England's policies. Reminiscent of his upbringing in County Down, Ireland, Alexander was again subject to British domination; and it wasn't to his liking.

Having made his home within the bounds of Fredericksville Parish,[24] Alexander's life would soon become an uncomfortable

---

[21] Robert F. Collins, *A History of the Daniel Boone National Forest* (Winchester, Kentucky: Robert F. Collins, 1975), 152; digital images, *Google Books* (http://www.books.google.com: 4 December 2018)
[22] Collins, *A History of the Daniel Boone National Forest*, 152.
[23] Louisa County Virginia," Louisa County, Virginia, Deed Book A and B, 1742-1759", Part 2: p. 326, Thomas Hackett to George Clark entry, 15 August 1748; Library of Virginia microfilm 1.

one. According to the Act of Toleration of 1689, to freely worship as a Presbyterian without penalty, one had to swear an oath of allegiance to the British government. If he refused, he could be fined or jailed.[25]

Required to *"solemnly declare before God and the world, that I will be true and faithful to King William and Queen Mary; and...that no foreign prince, person, prelate, state, or potentate, hath or ought to have, any power, jurisdiction, superiority, pre-eminence, or authority ecclesiastical or spiritual within this realm,"*[26] dissenters had to prove they were loyal English subjects. In addition, they had to *"process faith in God the Father, and in Jesus Christ His eternal Son, the true God, and in the Holy Spirit."*[27]

Worshiping with other like-minded individuals, Alexander was considered an outsider by the local Anglican congregation. Aligning himself with dissenters from all religious backgrounds, he placed in jeopardy his reputation and his freedom to live as he pleased. Preferring the company of Quakers, converted Anglicans, and Presbyterians, he formed close relationships with these dissenting pioneers. It was during this time that he became acquainted with Sarah Austin, who would become his first wife.

The childhoods of Alexander and Sarah couldn't be more different. While Alexander was a new arrival from Ireland, Sarah's family was already established in the colony. The daughter

---

[24] Louisa County, Virginia, "Louisa County, Virginia, Order Book 1744-1748", p. 235, Thomas Joyce Entry, July 28 1747; Library of Virginia, microfilm 29.

[25] Robert P. Davis, James H. Smylie, Dean K. Thompson, Ernest Trice Thompson, William Newton Todd, *Virginia Presbyterians in American Life: Hanover Presbytery (1755-1980)* (Richmond, Virginia: Hanover Presbytery, 1982), 5

[26] University of Wisconsin, *Act of Toleration, May 1689* (Wisconsin: University of Wisconsin), 1-2; digital images, *University of Wisconsin* (https://www.ssc.wisc.edu/~rkeyser/wp/wp-content/uploads/2015/06/TolerationAct1689.pdf: accessed 21 11 2017).

[27] University of Wisconsin, *Act of Toleration, May 1689*, 1-2.

of Richard Austin III, a landowner of Hanover County, Virginia,[28] she was a third-generation Virginian. Recorded as participating in St. Paul's Parish, Sarah's family had been raised in the Anglican Church.

Documentation of their marriage is now lost; however, as a Presbyterian who had been penalized by the Church of England's policies, Alexander would not have had any inclination to marry a faithful Anglican. With this background, it is probable that Sarah was a religious dissenter as well.

Blessed with the ability to form relationships with established and influential community leaders, Alexander understood how to rise in society. A man of ambition and integrity, he earned the respect of those that held political and economic power. It was this quality that enabled Alexander to become a significant contributor to one of Virginia's most historic and notable settlements in southern Virginia, Cub Creek.

On May 10, 1748, Alexander is recorded as buying eight-hundred acres of land in Lunenburg County, Virginia, from John Lidderdale, Alexander Spaulding, and Samuel Gordon.[29] Having gained the trust of these wealthy landowners from central Virginia, Alexander became part of one of the first migrations to the Presbyterian settlement of Cub Creek.[30] Contributing economically, politically, and ecclesiastically to the well-being of this dissenting settlement, he played a significant role in helping to

---

[28] Lunenburg County Virginia, *"Lunenburg County, Will Book No. 1, 1746-1762,"* p. 280-281, Richard Austin entry, 4 December 1759; Library of Virginia microfilm 19.

[29] Lunenburg County, Virginia, *"Lunenburg County, Virginia, Deed Book 1 & 2, 1746-1752,"* pt.1: P. 368-370, entry for Alexander Joyce, 1748; Library of Virginia, microfilm 1.

[30] Landon C. Bell, *Sunlight on the Southside: Lists of Tithes Lunenburg County, Virginia, 1748-1783* (1931; reprint, Baltimore, Maryland: Genealogical Publishing Co., Inc, 1974), 78.

build the foundation for the Presbyterian denomination in the southern colonies.[31]

As a settler on this new frontier, Alexander experienced opportunities not offered to religious dissenters in more developed areas. Permitted to worship according to Presbyterian doctrines with moderate restrictions, farm the best land available and participate in political affairs, he rose in social status. First and foremost in Alexander's mind, however, was his desire to experience religious tolerance.

From the time of his birth in Ireland, Alexander had faced political, economic, and religious persecution. As an adult, he was restless, ambitious, and determined to build a better life for himself and his family. Whether it was his toiling in the tobacco fields or his serving in public office, his childhood and experiences as a young adult changed him forever. These changes are best identified when he becomes a Presbyterian Ruling Elder.

Exactly how Alexander became a Presbyterian Elder is not known, but by December 3, 1755, he had become a respected ecclesiastical leader. Documented at the first meeting of the Presbytery of Hanover at Polegreen Church in Hanover County, Virginia,[32] Alexander was a crucial player in the struggle for religious tolerance.

Inspired by the piety and dedication of the Rev. Samuel Davies, the most well-known Presbyterian minister in Virginia, Alexander was encouraged to serve in ecclesiastical office. Recorded along with the Rev. Davies at the founding of Polegreen Church on

---

[31] Presbyterian Church in the U.S.; Hanover Minutes, 1755-1756; Union Presbyterian Seminary, microfilm.
[32] Presbyterian Church in the U.S.; Hanover Minutes, 1755-1756.

December 3, 1755,[33] he helped established the Presbyterian Church in Virginia.

Like most dissenting Christians in eighteenth-century Virginia, Alexander was more progressive than his Anglican neighbors. Concerned that the Church of England's worship services lacked an energizing element, he sought to *"increase the knowledge and influence"* of God *"in the hearts and lives of men"* by traveling to different communities in order to spread the Gospel.[34]

In addition to being a faithful participant at the Presbytery of Hanover meetings at Cub Creek Church and Buffalo Creek Church in Prince Edward, County,[35] Alexander likely supported the education of African American slaves. Although they *"were far from having money to purchase books, that they themselves [African-American Slaves] are [were] the property of others,"*[36] Alexander offered them a place of refuge within the Presbyterian denomination. Reacting enthusiastically to this mission, they were *"willing and eagerly desirous to be instructed, and[to] embrace every opportunity of acquainting themselves with the doctrines of the gospel."*[37]

Alexander's missionary work also extended to Native Americans. Following the example of the Rev. Samuel Davies, Alexander also likely embraced the idea of sending missionaries to the Catawba and Cherokee tribes.[38] Having offered the opportunity of being

---

[33] Samuel Davies, *Sermons on Important* Subjects (1810; Forgotten Books: 2012), V.
[34] Presbyterian Church in the U.S.; Hanover Minutes, 1755-1756.
[35] Rev. Samuel Davies, *Memoir of the Rev. Samuel* Davies (Massachusetts Sabbath School Society: Boston, Massachusetts,1832), 25.
[36] Rev. Samuel Davies, *Memoir of the Rev. Samuel* Davies (Massachusetts Sabbath School Society: Boston, Massachusetts,1832), 26.
[37] Rev. Samuel Davies, *Memoir of the Rev. Samuel* Davies (Massachusetts Sabbath School Society: Boston, Massachusetts,1832), 115.
[38] Rev. Samuel Davies, *Memoir of the Rev. Samuel* Davies (Massachusetts Sabbath School Society: Boston, Massachusetts,1832), 117.

provided with a Christian education, both nations agreed with this plan, welcoming one *"missionary and a schoolmaster."*[39]

It was during this period that Alexander's wife Sarah passed away. The cause of her death is not recorded; however, her marriage to Alexander was a fruitful one. She and Alexander had six children: Thomas Joyce,[40] John (Possum) Joyce[41], James Joyce,[42] Elijah Joyce,[43] Sarah Joyce,[44] and Alexander Joyce.[45]

---

[39] Corinne Johnson Murray, *The Joyces* (Corinne Johnson Murray: Greensboro, North Carolina), p. 5-6; Descendants of Thomas and Alexander Joyce Families Association, *Research Update on Wives of Alexander and Thomas Joyce,* 1-2; digital images, *Descendants of Thomas and Alexander Joyce Families Association (*https://www.thomasandalexanderjoyceassociation.com/research-updates: accessed 18 3 2019); Guilford County, North Carolina, "*Record of Wills 1771-1942, index, 1772-1934*," 3 March 1778; digital image, North Carolina County, District and Probate Courts, Ancestry (http://www.ancestry.com: accessed 10 October 2016).

[40] Murray, *The Joyces*, p. 5-6; Descendants of Thomas and Alexander Joyce Families Association, *Research Update on Wives of Alexander and Thomas Joyce,* 1-2; Guilford County, North Carolina, "Record of Wills 1771-1943, index, 1772-1934," 3 March 1778.

[41] Murray, *The Joyces*, p. 5-6; Descendants of Thomas and Alexander Joyce Families Association, *Research Update on Wives of Alexander and Thomas Joyce,* 1-2; Guilford County, North Carolina, "Record of Wills 1771-1943, index, 1772-1934," 3 March 1778.

[42] Murray, *The Joyces*, p. 5-6; Descendants of Thomas and Alexander Joyce Families Association, *Research Update on Wives of Alexander and Thomas Joyce,* 1-2; Guilford County, North Carolina, "Record of Wills 1771-1943, index, 1772-1934," 3 March 1778.

[43] Murray, *The Joyces*, 3; Descendants of Thomas and Alexander Joyce Families Association, *Research Update on Wives of Alexander and Thomas Joyce,* 1-2; Guilford County, North Carolina, "Record of Wills 1771-1943, index, 1772-1934," 3 March 1778.

[44] Murray, *The Joyces*, 26; Descendants of Thomas and Alexander Joyce Families Association, *Research Update on Wives of Alexander and Thomas Joyce,* 1-2; Guilford County, North Carolina, "Record of Wills 1771-1943, index, 1772-1934," 3 March 1778.

[45] Prince Edward County, Virginia, "*Prince Edward County, Virginia, Virginia, Marriage Bonds, 1754-1850*," Alexander Joyce to Jane Hamilton."; Library of Virginia.

In 1760, two years after Sarah's death, Alexander married Jane Hamilton at Buffalo Creek Church in Prince Edward County, Virginia.[46] Children born to Alexander and Jane were Esther Joyce,[47] Elisha Joyce,[48] Andrew Joyce,[49] Robert Joyce,[50] Margaret Joyce,[51] Elizabeth Joyce,[52] and Mary Joyce.[53]

In addition to his other accomplishments, Alexander also became a surveyor. Trusted by the local Cornwall Parish, he was given the responsibility of building and maintaining many of the major roads in the area. Beginning on October 31, 1753, he was ordered

---

[46] Murray, *The Joyces*, p. 27; Descendants of Thomas and Alexander Joyce Families Association, *Research Update on Wives of Alexander and Thomas Joyce*, 1-2; Guilford County, North Carolina, "Record of Wills 1771-1943, index, 1772-1934," 3 March 1778.

[47] Murray, *The Joyces*, p. 23; Descendants of Thomas and Alexander Joyce Families Association, *Research Update on Wives of Alexander and Thomas Joyce*, 1-2; Guilford County, North Carolina, "Record of Wills 1771-1943, index, 1772-1934," 3 March 1778.

[48] Murray, *The Joyces*, 26; Descendants of Thomas and Alexander Joyce Families Association, *Research Update on Wives of Alexander and Thomas Joyce*, 1-2; Guilford County, North Carolina, "Record of Wills 1771-1943, index, 1772-1934," 3 March 1778.

[49] Murray, *The Joyces*, 26; Descendants of Thomas and Alexander Joyce Families Association, *Research Update on Wives of Alexander and Thomas Joyce*, 1-2; Guilford County, North Carolina, "Record of Wills 1771-1943, index, 1772-1934," 3 March 1778.

[50] Murray, *The Joyces*, 3; Descendants of Thomas and Alexander Joyce Families Association, *Research Update on Wives of Alexander and Thomas Joyce*, 1-2; Guilford County, North Carolina, "Record of Wills 1771-1943, index, 1772-1934," 3 March 1778.

[51] Murray, *The Joyces*, 27; Descendants of Thomas and Alexander Joyce Families Association, *Research Update on Wives of Alexander and Thomas Joyce*, 1-2; Guilford County, North Carolina, "Record of Wills 1771-1943, index, 1772-1934," 3 March 1778.

[52] Murray, *The Joyces*, 27; Descendants of Thomas and Alexander Joyce Families Association, *Research Update on Wives of Alexander and Thomas Joyce*, 1-2; Guilford County, North Carolina, "Record of Wills 1771-1943, index, 1772-1934," 3 March 1778.

[53] Nathaniel Mason Pawlett, Tyler Jefferson Boyd Research Assistant, *Lunenburg County Road orders 1746-1764* (Charlottesville, Virginia: Virginia Transportation Research Council, 2004), 65.

"*to lay open and Clear a Road from Little Ronoke Bridge to the head of the south branch of Wards ford Creek.*"[54] Over the following years, he continued to be relied above upon for important road construction projects.

On November 5, 1755, Alexander and Richard Austin were ordered to clear *"the best & most Convenientest Way from the County line near William Watsons to Cubb Creek Road near John Wallers."*[55] Two years later, on March 1, 1757, Alexander and Joseph Morton were *"to Assist the Surveyor of the Road leading from Little Roanoak Bridge to the County, as they shall think Proper."*[56] On February 9, 1764, Alexander received a reward for his contributions by having a road named in his honor. After surveying a road near *"Alexander Joyces Road,"*[57] we find that his name was well-known in the area. Despite his many accomplishments, he did not stay in Virginia and is later documented as buying land in Rowan County, North Carolina.

On May 16, 1760, Alexander purchased land on Shepperd's Creek in North Carolina from James Shepperd.[58] On March 3, 1778, he passed away at fifty-eight years of age in Guilford County, North Carolina.[59] Today known as Joyce Country, his descendants

---

[54] Nathaniel Mason Pawlett, Tyler Jefferson Boyd Research Assistant, *Lunenburg County Road orders 1746-1764* (Charlottesville, Virginia: Virginia Transportation Research Council, 2004), 87

[55] Nathaniel Mason Pawlett, Tyler Jefferson Boyd Research Assistant, *Lunenburg County Road orders 1746-1764* (Charlottesville, Virginia: Virginia Transportation Research Council, 2004), 95.

[56] Nathaniel Mason Pawlett, Tyler Jefferson Boyd Research Assistant, *Lunenburg County Road orders 1746-1764* (Charlottesville, Virginia: Virginia Transportation Research Council, 2004), 163.

[57] Ibid

[58] "Alexander Joyce (1720-1778) 1778 Will: Part 1-2," March 1778, *Descendants of Alexander and Thomas Joyce Families Association*, Documentation

[59] Murray, The Joyces, p. 5-6; Descendants of Thomas and Alexander Joyce Families Association, *Research Update on Wives of Alexander and Thomas Joyce, 1-2*; Guilford County, North Carolina, "Record of Wills 1771-1942, index, 1772-1934," 3 March 1778.

populate several areas of Rockingham and Stokes Counties, North Carolina. From his trials and tribulations in County Down, Ireland to his rise in social status in the New World, Alexander helped make Virginia what it is today.

**Children**

The children of Alexander Joyce and Sarah Austin are as follows:

- **Thomas Joyce:** Born circa 1743 around Louisa County, Virginia;[60] died in 1822 in Rockingham County, Virginia.[61] He married Margaret "Peggy" Tate.[62]
- **John (Possum) Joyce**: Born circa 1743 around Louisa County, Virginia;[63] died in February of 1828 in Rockingham County, North Carolina.[64] He married Peggy.[65]

---

[60] Corinne Johnson Murray, *The Joyces* (Corinne Johnson Murray: Greensboro, North Carolina), 6.
[61] Murry, *The Joyces*, 6.
[62] Murray, *The Joyces*, p. 5-6; Descendants of Thomas and Alexander Joyce Families Association, *Research Update on Wives of Alexander and Thomas Joyce*, 1-2; Guilford County, North Carolina, "Record of Wills 1771-1943, index, 1772-1934," 3 March 1778.
[63] Corinne Johnson Murray, *The Joyces* (Corinne Johnson Murray: Greensboro, North Carolina), 10.
[64] Murry, *The Joyces*, 10.
[65] Corinne Johnson Murray, *The Joyces* (Corinne Johnson Murray: Greensboro, North Carolina), p.16; Descendants of Thomas and Alexander Joyce Families Association, *Research Update on Wives of Alexander and Thomas Joyce, 1-2*; Guilford County, North Carolina, "Record of Wills 1771-1943, index, 1772-1934," 3 March 1778.

- **James Joyce**: Born in 1746 in Louisa County, Virginia;⁶⁶ died 1796 in Rockingham County, North Carolina.⁶⁷
- **Elijah Joyce**: Born May 19, 1752, in Lunenburg County, Virginia;⁶⁸ died 1804 in Rockingham County, North Carolina. He married Elizabeth Allen.⁶⁹
- **Sarah Joyce**: Born 1750 in Lunenburg County, Virginia;⁷⁰ death date unknown. She married Joel Mackey on March 24, 1772.⁷¹
- **Alexander Joyce**: Born in the 1740s in Virginia;⁷² died about 1837 in Georgia.⁷³ He married Francis Hicks, widow of James Hicks.⁷⁴

---

⁶⁶ Murry, *The Joyces*, 16.

⁶⁷ Corinne Johnson Murray, *The Joyces* (Corinne Johnson Murray: Greensboro, North Carolina), p.18; Descendants of Thomas and Alexander Joyce Families Association, *Research Update on Wives of Alexander and Thomas Joyce, 1-2*; Guilford County, North Carolina, "Record of Wills 1771-1943, index, 1772-1934," 3 March 1778.

⁶⁸ Murry, *The Joyces*, 19.

⁶⁹ Murray, *The Joyces*, 26; Descendants of Thomas and Alexander Joyce Families Association, *Research Update on Wives of Alexander and Thomas Joyce,* 1-2; Guilford County, North Carolina, "Record of Wills 1771-1943, index, 1772-1934," 3 March 1778.

⁷⁰ Murray, *The Joyces*, 26.

⁷¹ C.T. Joyce and Marion Joyce, *On the Waters of Spring Creek: Descendants of James and Mary Epperson Joyce* (2018), 1; Descendants of Thomas and Alexander Joyce Families Association, *Research Update on Wives of Alexander and Thomas Joyce,* 1-2; Guilford County, North Carolina, "Record of Wills 1771-1943, index, 1772-1934," 3 March 1778.

⁷² Joyce, *On the Waters of Spring Creek: Descendants of James and Mary Epperson Joyce*, 1.

⁷³ Ibid

⁷⁴ Corinne Johnson Murray, *The Joyces* (Corinne Johnson Murray : Greensboro, North Carolina), 27; Descendants of Thomas and Alexander Joyce Families Association, *Research Update on Wives of Alexander and Thomas Joyce,* 1-2; Guilford County, North Carolina, "Record of Wills 1771-1943, index, 1772-1934," 3 March 1778.

The children of Alexander Joyce and Sarah Hamilton are as follows:

- **Esther Joyce:** Born August 20, 1760;[75] died March 20, 1812, in Surry County, North Carolina.[76] She married John Bryson.[77]
- **Elisha Joyce**: Born August 9, 1872;[78] died September 14, 1825, in Rockingham County, North Carolina.[79] He married Sarah Shackelford on December 31, 1782.[80]
- **Andrew Joyce**: Born 1765;[81] died before 1850.[82] He married Elizabeth King in Henry County, Virginia on January 24, 1792.[83]
- **Robert Joyce**: Born March 21, 1768;[84] died January 22, 1814, in Patrick County, Virginia.[85] He married Elizabeth Lindsay.[86]

---

[75] Murray, *The Joyces*, 27.
[76] Ibid
[77] Corinne Johnson Murray, *The Joyces* (Corinne Johnson Murray: Greensboro, North Carolina), 23; Descendants of Thomas and Alexander Joyce Families Association, *Research Update on Wives of Alexander and Thomas Joyce,* 1-2; Guilford County, North Carolina, "Record of Wills 1771-1943, index, 1772-1934," 3 March 1778.
[78] Murray, *The Joyces*, 23.
[79] Ibid
[80] Murray, *The Joyces*, 26; Descendants of Thomas and Alexander Joyce Families Association, *Research Update on Wives of Alexander and Thomas Joyce,* 1-2; Guilford County, North Carolina, "Record of Wills 1771-1943, index, 1772-1934," 3 March 1778.
[81] Murray, *The Joyces*, 26.
[82] Ibid
[83] Murray, *The Joyces*, 26; Descendants of Thomas and Alexander Joyce Families Association, *Research Update on Wives of Alexander and Thomas Joyce,* 1-2; Guilford County, North Carolina, "Record of Wills 1771-1943, index, 1772-1934," 3 March 1778.
[84] Murray, *The Joyces*, 26
[85] Ibid

- **Margaret Joyce**: Born April 21, 1770, in North Carolina;[87] died October 31, 1848, in Lincoln County, Tennessee.[88] She married John Gibson.[89]
- **Elizabeth Joyce**: Born November 8, 1772, in Rockingham County, North Carolina;[90] died Davidson County, Tennessee.[91] She married Newsome Barham on July 22, 1794.[92]
- **Mary Joyce:** Born September 4, 1775;[93] died November 28, 1815.[94]

---

[86] Find a Grave.* *Find a Grave*, database with images (http://www.findagrave.com: accessed 26 April 2019), memorial 40086721, Mrs. Margaret Joyce Gibson (death 1848), Gibson Cemetery, Lincoln County, Tennessee; gravestone photograph by Jimbo; Murray, *The Joyces*, 26; Guilford County, North Carolina, "Record of Wills 1771-1943, index, 1772-1934," 3 March 1778.

[87] *Find a Grave*, memorial 40086721, Mrs. Margaret Joyce Gibson (death 1848), gravestone photograph by Jimbo.

[88] *Find a Grave*, memorial 40086721, Mrs. Margaret Joyce Gibson (death 1848), gravestone photograph by Jimbo; Murray, *The Joyces*, 27.

[89] Murray, *The Joyces*, 27; Guilford County, North Carolina, "Record of Wills 1771-1943, index, 1772-1934," 3 March 1778; Descendants of Thomas and Alexander Joyce Families Association, *Research Update on Wives of Alexander and Thomas Joyce,* 1-2.

[90] John Bennett Boddie, *Historical Southern Families* (Pacific Coast Publishers: 1964), 151; digital books, *Google Books* (http://www.books.google.com: accessed 26 April 2019).

[91] Boddie, *Historical Southern Families*, 151.

[92] Murray, *The Joyces*, 27; Guilford County, North Carolina, "Record of Wills 1771-1943, index, 1772-1934," 3 March 1778; Descendants of Thomas and Alexander Joyce Families Association, *Research Update on Wives of Alexander and Thomas Joyce,* 1-2.

[93] Murray, *The Joyces*, 27; Guilford County, North Carolina, "Record of Wills 1771-1943, index, 1772-1934," 3 March 1778; Descendants of Thomas and Alexander Joyce Families Association, *Research Update on Wives of Alexander and Thomas Joyce,* 1-2.

[94] Murray, *The Joyces*, 27.

## Conclusion

From the earliest years of the colony of Virginia, the survival of the New World depended upon brave pioneers to settle on the frontier. From indentured servants, wealthy landowners, refugees, to religious dissenters, all sorts of adventurers accepted this challenge. However, these were not the only forces responsible for expanding the colony. Religious denominations and government institutions also were interested in settling and reshaping this new land. One of these groups, the Presbyterian Church, played an important role. Under the leadership of itinerant ministers and elders, the ecclesiastical policies of colonial Virginia were challenged and reshaped by this influential faith group. Over time, its mission to spark a spiritual enlightenment would have far-reaching political consequences. One of its leaders, Alexander Joyce, although not widely-known, played a crucial role in how the colony developed.

Born in County Down, Ireland in a time of great political and religious strife, Alexander experienced significant hardship. Emigrating to the New World, likely in the early 1740s, he arrived most likely in Pennsylvania but shortly afterward migrated farther inland to Louisa County, Virginia, where he became part of the local Scots-Irish, Presbyterian community. This experience, however, proved to be somewhat of a disappointment. Faced again with religious and political persecution, he purchased land and moved farther south to Lunenburg County, Virginia, where he became involved in the Presbyterian Church. Documented as assisting in the founding of the Presbyterian denomination in Virginia, Alexander became a champion for religious tolerance. A likely supporter of the Christian education of African slaves, he believed that they, too, should experience spiritual enlightenment. By the time he retired, he had purchased land in North Carolina, and had become one of the wealthiest and most influential settlers in Lunenburg County. At the time of his death in 1778, most of his children had moved to Rockingham County, North Carolina; where many of his descendants continue to reside today.

- The son of Thomas Joyce and Mary Blaikley,[95] Alexander was born in 1720 in County Down, Ireland.[96]
- Because of severe economic deprivation, political persecution and religious persecution in Ireland, Alexander and his family suffered greatly under British rule. Restricting the trade of wool to England and Wales, the income of weavers was severely affected,[97] reducing the condition of workers to poverty. Alexander and his family suffered under the effects of this financial downturn.
- In a time of *"Reoccurring bad harvests,"*[98] landlords *"doubled or trebled"* their rent.[99] Because of these conditions, Alexander was forced to emigrate to the New World for better opportunities
- In 1740, during the year of the slaughter, County Down, Ireland was *"almost emptied of their [its] protestant inhabitants."*[100] With virtually no prospects left for a good life in Ireland, Alexander set sail for America, most likely for Pennsylvania.
- Included among the *"great numbers"* of Scots-Irish that flocked to Pennsylvania,[101] he was a participant

---

[95] Davies, "Welcome to People's Names of Co. Down, Ireland," *Ros Davies' Co. Down, Northern Ireland Family Research Site*, entry for Thomas Joyce and Mary Blaikley.
[96] Davies, "Welcome to People's Names of Co. Down, Ireland," *Ros Davies' Co. Down, Northern Ireland Family Research Site* entry for Alexander Joyce baptized January 1720.
[97] Dunaway, *The Scotch-Irish of Colonial Pennsylvania*, 29.
[98] Dunaway, *The Scotch-Irish of Colonial Pennsylvania*, 30.
[99] Dunaway, *The Scotch-Irish of Colonial Pennsylvania*, 29.
[100] Dunaway, *The Scotch-Irish of Colonial Pennsylvania*, 40.
[101] Griffin, *The People with No Name: Ireland's Ulster Scots, America's Scots-Irish, And the Creation of a British Atlantic World 1689-1764*, 101.

in a historic immigration. Like the experiences of other Scots-Irish settlers, he felt the condemnation of many of the colony's Native inhabitants that *"feared that the swarms of Irish and Germans would transform the province beyond recognition and imperil their position in society."*[102]

- Alexander did not stay in Pennsylvania for long, and he is next documented in Louisa County, Virginia, as a witness to a land transaction in Fredericksville Parish dated August 15, 1748.[103] Here he joined the local Scots-Irish community. Despite finding a community of like-minded individuals, he once again found himself a target for political and religious persecution.
- Considered a religious dissenter by the Church of England, Alexander was required to take an oath of allegiance before he could worship as a Presbyterian.[104] If he refused, he could be fined or jailed.[105]
- On May 10, 1748, Alexander bought eight-hundred acres of land in Lunenburg County, Virginia and became part of the Scots-Irish community of Cub Creek.[106] One the first participants in this historic southern migration, he settled on Ward's Fork.[107]

---

[102] Ibid

[103] Louisa County Virginia," Louisa County, Virginia, Deed Book A and B, 1742-1759", Part 2: p. 326, Thomas Hackett to George Clark entry, 15 August 1748; Louisa County, Virginia, "Louisa County, Virginia, Order Book 1744-1748", p. 235, Thomas Joyce Entry, July 28 1747

[104] University of Wisconsin, *Act of Toleration, May 1689*, 1-2

[105] Davis, Smylie, Thompson, Thompson, Todd, *Virginia Presbyterians in American Life: Hanover Presbytery (1755-1980)*, 5.

[106] Lunenburg County, Virginia, "*Lunenburg County, Virginia, Deed Book 1 & 2, 1746-1752*," pt.1: P. 368-370, entry for Alexander Joyce,

[107] Bell, *Sunlight on the Southside: Lists of Tithes Lunenburg County, Virginia, 1748-1783*, 78.

- Granted freedoms not customarily given to religious dissenters, Alexander quickly rose in social status. He was allowed to worship according to his faith with moderate restrictions and contributed to the well-being of the Presbyterian denomination. In time, he became one of the most influential ecclesiastical leaders in the area.
- By December 3, 1755, Alexander had become a respected elder within the Presbyterian Church.[108] Recorded with prominent Presbyterian leaders at the founding of the Presbytery of Hanover at Polegreen Church in Hanover County, Virginia, he and his colleagues played an essential role in the establishment and spreading Presbyterianism in the south. Alexander continued to be documented as a Ruling Elder at Buffalo Creek Church in Prince Edward County, Virginia on September 24, 1760,[109] and at Cub Creek Church on October 15, 1766.[110]
- A likely supporter of educating slaves, Native Americans, and the disenfranchised, Alexander believed that *"the knowledge and influence"* of God should be taught to everyone.[111] Concerned that they *"were far from having money to purchase books, that they themselves [African-American Slaves] are [were] the property of others,"*[112] he labored to provide them a place of spiritual refuge within the Presbyterian Church.

---

[108] Presbyterian Church in the U.S.; Hanover Minutes, 1755-1756.
[109] Ibid
[110] Ibid
[111] Davies, *Sermons on Important* Subjects, v; Davies, *Memoir of the Rev. Samuel Davies,* 115.
[112] Davies, *Sermons on Important* Subjects, v; Davies, *Memoir of the Rev. Samuel Davies,* 25.

- Alexander was also a successful surveyor. He was trusted by Cornwall Parish to survey, build and maintain many of the major roads in Lunenburg County, Virginia. On October 31, 1753, he was ordered *"to lay open and Clear a Road from Little Ronoke Bridge to the head of the south branch of Wards ford Creek."*[113] Later on November 5, 1755, he and Richard Austin were ordered to clear *"the best & most Convenientest Way from the County line near William Watsons to Cubb Creek Road near John Wallers."*[114] Finally, he was rewarded for his hard work, when a road in Lunenburg County was named in his honor, around 1764.[115]
- After moving to North Carolina, Alexander passed away on March 3, 1778, in Guilford County,[116] leaving behind thirteen children.[117] His lineage and achievements continue to be lovingly remembered and proudly honored by his descendants.

---

[113] Pawlett, Boyd, *Lunenburg County Road orders 1746-1764*, 65.
[114] Pawlett, Boyd, *Lunenburg County Road orders 1746-1764*, 87.
[115] Pawlett, Boyd, *Lunenburg County Road orders 1746-1764*, 163.
[116] "Alexander Joyce (1720-1778) 1778 Will: Part 1-2," March 1778, *Descendants of Alexander and Thomas Joyce Families Association*, Documentation.
[117] Guilford County, North Carolina, "Record of Wills 1771-1943, index, 1772-1934," 3 March 1778.

# Chapter 3
# David Barrow

From the beginning of the United States, slavery was a controversial matter. Embedded in the economic, political, and ecclesiastical foundations of the newly-formed country, it had become a staple of southern life. While this system provided a standard of living for those in power, it also legalized the immoral ownership of human beings. However, because of its economic benefits, slave-owning landowners embraced it as a fact of life.

There were dissenting voices, however. The Rev. David Barrow, a staunch opponent of slavery, persisted in preaching against the immorality of slavery, and in support of emancipation. Risking his life, he helped establish the first anti-slavery association in Kentucky. By the time of his death, David Barrow had become one of the leading advocates in America in the fight for emancipation.

**David's Parentage**: The son of William Barrow and Amey Lee,[1] he grew up in Brunswick County, Virginia.

**David Barrow**: Born October 10, 1753, in Brunswick County, Virginia;[2] died November 19, 1819, in Montgomery County, Kentucky.[3] He married Sarah Gillam on April 6, 1773.[4]

---

[1] Mae Belle Barrow North, *The Barrow Family of Virginia: 1620-1972* (Golden Triangle Printing Co. of Greensboro: Greensboro, North Carolina, 1972), 186; University of Kentucky, *Bureau of School Bulletin: 1970-1971* (University of Kentucky: Ohio, 1970), 19.

**Life Story**: The life of David Barrow began humbly. Raised on his father's farm in Brunswick county, Virginia, he became accustomed to planting and harvesting tobacco, Indian corn, and other crops. Having had little access to educational opportunities, he found it difficult to rise in social status. However, he always maintained a curiosity and an *"ambitious zeal"* that would ultimately lead him into a new life.[5]

During his formative years, David was aware of the religious and political strife stirring in Virginia. The Church of England held supreme power as both church and state, and those that dissented from the Church risked being fined or jailed.[6] Required to take oaths of allegiance, these nonconformists *"solemnly declare[d] before God and the world, that I[they] will be true and faithful to King William and Queen Mary; and…that no foreign prince, person, prelate, state, or potentate, hath or ought to have, any power, jurisdiction, superiority, pre-eminence, or authority ecclesiastical or spiritual within this realm."*[7] In addition, they had to *"process faith in God the Father, and in Jesus Christ His eternal Son, the true God, and in the Holy Spirit."*[8]

---

[2] North, *The Barrow Family of Virginia: 1620-1972*,186; University of Kentucky, *Bureau of School Bulletin: 1970-1971*, 19.

[3] University of Kentucky, *Bureau of School Bulletin: 1970-1971*, 19.

[4] University of Kentucky, *Bureau of School Bulletin: 1970-1971*, 19; Plainfield-Guilford Township Public Library, *Barrow PDF* (Plainfield-Guilford Township Public Library: Plainfield, Indiana), 5; digital images, Digitized Family History Files (http://www.plainfieldlibrary.net/wp-content/uploads/2015/03/Barrow.pdf: accessed 9 January 2019).

[5] University of Kentucky, *Bureau of School Bulletin: 1970-1971*, 19.

[6] Robert P. Davis, James H. Smylie, Dean K. Thompson, Ernest Trice Thompson, William Newton Todd, *Virginia Presbyterians in American Life: Hanover Presbytery (1755-1980)* (Richmond, Virginia: Hanover Presbytery, 1982), 5

[7] University of Wisconsin, *Act of Toleration, May 1689* (Wisconsin: University of Wisconsin), 1-2; digital images, *University of Wisconsin* (https://www.ssc.wisc.edu/~rkeyser/wp/wp-content/uploads/2015/06/TolerationAct1689.pdf: accessed 21 11 2017).

[8] University of Wisconsin, *Act of Toleration, May 1689*, 1-2.

As a member of the Church of England,[9] David learned that religious tests were not the only reason the Church was losing members. Considered to be impersonal by the dissenting denominations, Anglican sermons could not compete with the popularity of more charismatic Presbyterian ministers. Attracted to the zealous and energetic sermons of pastors such as the Rev. Samuel Davies whose sermons *"increase[d] the knowledge and influence"* of God *"in the hearts and lives of men,"*[10] David came to embrace this ant-Anglican sentiment.

Additionally, spiritual discontent, accompanied by the controversies of oppressive tax laws, helped reshape David's world view. Observing that the natural born rights of Englishmen were being violated, he watched as his father, William Barrow, struggled to pay for paint, paper, lead, glass, tea, and other necessities.[11] It was during this time that, *"9 percent of the nation's income"* was helping Great Britain with a 130 million-pound debt.[12]

At sixteen years of age, David became spiritually and politically active. Having become disillusioned with the Church of England and the British government, he decided to become a dissenter himself. Risking his reputation, he was *"baptized by Zachariah Thompson into Fountain Creek Church."*[13] Officially becoming a Baptist, David Barrow began his tutorage under Pastor Zachariah Thompson guidance.

---

[9] John Bennett Boddie, Births, Deaths and Sponsers 1717-1778 From the Albemarle Parish Register (Baltimore, Maryland: Genealogical Publishing Co., 1998), 86.

[10] Samuel Davies, *Sermons on Important* Subjects (1810; Forgotten Books: , 2012), V.

[11] Danby Pickering, *The Avalon Project: Documents in Law, History, and Diplomacy* (http://avalon.law.yale.edu/18th_century/townsend_act_1767.asp: accessed 24 May 2018), "The Townsend Act."

[12] Nick Bunker, *An Empire on the Edge: How Britain came to Fight America* (New York, New York: Alfred A. Knopf, 2014), 29; digital images, *Google Books* (http://www.books.google.com: accessed 21 May 2018).

[13] University of Kentucky, *Bureau of School Bulletin: 1970-1971*, 19.

David and his mentor, Reverend Thompson, shared a similar religious upbringing. As a child, Zachariah *"poffeffed rare and fingular talent."*[14] Born into a working-class family, he had *"very little education,"*[15] but was *"fond of reading and improving his mind."*[16] Choosing a new path for himself, he *"embraced vital religion; and, being baptized, foon began to preach."*[17]

During the following three years, David learned several important lessons from Pastor Thompson. Embracing the concept of the Trinity, David *"believe[d] in only one indivisible, eternal, all-wise, all-powerful, all-holy, all-just, all-good, self-existing, self-governed, omniscient, omnipresent God ; and that in Deity there are three Divine Personalities different in character and office, but strictly One in design, nature, and essence, the Father, the Son, and the Holy Ghost."*[18]

A believer in the *"inspiration and infallibility of the Holy Scriptures,"*[19] David adopted a pro-Arminian stance on the nature of sin. In a time when Presbyterians were preaching that people were predestined to be saved, Baptists were teaching that, *"man was created in a state of innocency, but through the seduction of Satan, [and] being left to his own natural powers, fell into transgression,"*[20] and that they still could be *"influenced thereto by the power operations of the Divine Spirit"*[21] and be saved.

---

[14] Robert Baylor Semple, *A History of the Rise and Progress of the Baptists in Virginia* (Richmond, Virginia: Published by the author, 1810), 385; digital images, *Google Books* (http://www.books.google.com: accessed 15 January 2019).

[15] Sempe, *A History of the Rise and Progress of the Baptists in Virginia*, 385.

[16] Ibid

[17] Ibid

[18] James B. Taylor, *Virginia Baptist Ministers* (Philadelphia, Pennsylvania: J. B. Lippiincott & Co.,1859), 167; digital images, *Google Books* (http://www.books.google.com: accessed 15 January 2019).

[19] Taylor, *Virginia Baptist Ministers*, 167

[20] Ibid

[21] Ibid

David's political views also were reshaped under the mentorship of Pastor Thompson. Believing in *"the natural equality of man, except in some monstrous cases,"*[22] David came to embrace a stance on human rights that was viewed by many as highly unconventional. Accepting that liberty *"is the unalienable privilege of all men who have not forfeited those blessings by their own personal misdemeanors,"*[23] he condemned slavery as a *"curse."*[24]

This wasn't his only controversial position. Openly rejecting *"all religious tests"*[25] he began to preach against the *"oppressive"* attendance and tithe regulations of the Church of England.[26] Now a full-fledged religious dissenter, David Barrow looked back on his Anglican upbringing with remorse.

In 1773 David married Sarah Gillam,[27] and was ordained a Baptist minister.[28] Two years later, in 1774, he was invited to become a pastor at Mill Swamp Church in Isle of Wight County, Virginia.[29] However, ecclesiastical controversies soon followed that would challenge David and his convections.

Previously considered a stable denomination, disagreements began to arise within the Baptist Church. As an orthodox Baptist, David

---

[22] James B. Taylor, *Virginia Baptist Ministers* (Philadelphia, Pennsylvania: J. B. Lippiincott & Co.,1859), 169; digital images, *Google Books* (http://www.books.google.com: accessed 15 January 2019).
[23] Taylor, *Virginia Baptist Ministers*, 169.
[24] Rev. David Barrow, *Rev. David Barrow's Journal* (Winston-Salem, North Carolina: Wake Forest University); digital images, *ZSR Library* (https://wakespace.lib.wfu.edu/bitstream/handle/10339/62675/David_Barrow_journal.pdf?sequence=1: accessed 15 January 2019).
[25] Taylor, *Virginia Baptist Ministers*, 169.
[26] Ibid
[27] Plainfield-Guilford Township Public Library, *Barrow PDF.*
[28] William Elsey Connelley, E. M. Coulter, Ph. D., *History of Kentucky* (Chicago and New York: The American Historical Society, 1992), 310; digital image, *Google Books* (http://www.books.google.com: accessed 15 January 2019).
[29] Connelley, Coulter, *History of Kentucky*, 310.

believed that only *"orderly professing believer[s]"* could be baptized.[30] In contrast, opposing Free-Will Baptists thought that anyone could be baptized *"without requiring an experience of grace previous to their baptism."*[31] As a minister of the Kehukee Regular Baptist Association at Mill Swamp Church, David's appointment was not an easy one.

During his time of service, David was faced with skepticism and much opposition. Although he was *"unanimously invited"* to become pastor,[32] the Mill Swamp community was constituted of Free-Will Baptists.[33] Dedicated to reforming his church into the *"orthodox plan,"*[34] his efforts became so successful that Mill Swamp Church was where his ministry was *"most favored"* for years to come.[35] His work, however, soon was interrupted by the American Revolution.

The political, ecclesiastical, and economic conflicts surrounding the War for Independence forced David to choose a side. Fueled by his desire for religious and political liberties, he felt honor bound to fight for the Patriots. His service in the war is not

---

[30] James B. Taylor, *Virginia Baptist Ministers* (Philadelphia, Pennsylvania: J. B. Lippiincott & Co.,1859), 168; digital images, *Google Books* (http://www.books.google.com: accessed 15 January 2019).

[31] Elder Lemuel Burkitt, James Read, *A Concise History of the Kehukee Association, from its Original Rise Down to 1803* (Philadelphia, Pennsylvania: Lippiincott, Grambo and Co., 1850), 32; digital images, Google Books (http://www.books.google.com: accessed 19 January 2019).

[32] James B. Taylor, *Virginia Baptist Ministers* (Philadelphia, Pennsylvania: J. B. Lippiincott & Co.,1859), 155; digital images, *Google Books* (http://www.books.google.com: accessed 22 January 2019).

[33] Elder Lemuel Burkitt, James Read, *A Concise History of the Kehukee Association, from its Original Rise Down to 1803* (Philadelphia, Pennsylvania: Lippiincott, Grambo and Co., 1850), 276; digital images, Google Books (http://www.books.google.com: accessed 22 January 2019).

[34] Connelley, Coulter, *History of Kentucky*, 310.

[35] James B. Taylor, *Virginia Baptist Ministers* (Philadelphia, Pennsylvania: J. B. Lippiincott & Co.,1859), 162; digital images, *Google Books* (http://www.books.google.com: accessed 22 January 2019).

recorded; however, it was said he *"did a good service for his country, winning great honor for himself."*[36]

During the war, he acknowledged that slavery would not be abolished if the Americans won. Despite his condemnation of the slave trade, he maintained his commitment to the Patriotic cause. However, he did not forfeit his opposition to slavery, and after the war, he was again active in the abolitionist movement.

By 1778 David had become the pastor at Black Creek Church in Southampton County, Virginia.[37] His abolitionist activities there, however, were not as easily received as they were at Mill Swamp Church. Although he convinced *"at least three church members to free their slaves,"*[38] the majority of his congregation remained unpersuaded. With the slave trade solidly established as an essential part of Virginia's economy, David recognized his task would not be easy.

It was also in 1778 that David almost became a martyr. Accustomed to the jeers and criticisms of slaveowners, he was aware that his abolitionist views were putting his life at risk. After being invited to preach at a house in Southampton County, Virginia, he quickly found his life in danger. During one of his sermons, he was *"seized by a gang of ruffians"* and *"dragged a mile-half."*[39] Plunging his head into muddy water twice, they asked

---

[36] Connelley, Coulter, *History of Kentucky*, 310.

[37] Patrick H. Breen, *The Land Shall be Deluged in Blood: A New History of the Nat Turner Revolt* (Oxford, England: Oxford University Press, 2015), 155; digital images, *Google Books* (http://www.books.google.com: accessed 29 January 2019).

[38] Patrick H. Breen, *The Land Shall be Deluged in Blood: A New History of the Nat Turner Revolt* (Oxford, England: Oxford University Press, 2015), 156; digital images, *Google Books* (http://www.books.google.com: accessed 29 January 2019).

[39] Connelley, Coulter, *History of Kentucky*, 310, *The Baptist Encyclopedia* (Philadelphia, Pennsylvania: Louis H. Everts, 1881), 83; digital images, *Google Books* (http://www.books.google.com: accessed 31 January 2019).

"*if he believed.*"[40] Upon answering, "*I believe you are going to drown me,*"[41] they did not drown him but forced him to leave the area.

This traumatic experience, however, did not prevent David from pursuing his ministry. In 1784 he freed his slaves, and for the next fourteen years continued to preach in Virginia.[42] By 1798, however, he and his family had moved to Montgomery County, Kentucky.[43] Before doing so, he published a letter that detailed the reasons for his decision.

Unafraid of "*temptations and trails,*"[44] he was more troubled about the conflict of interest between his ministry and using slaves to maintain a farm. He also wanted to raise his children in an environment where they would not be shunned by slaveowners.

From the beginning, David had a thriving ministry in Kentucky. He became pastor at Mount Sterling Church, Goshen, and Lullebegrud Baptist Church,[45] and established a school for children.[46] As an educator, he understood the importance of establishing such an institution on the frontier. In addition to serving an essential role as a pastor, David now could support his family as a paid teacher.[47]

---

[40] Connelley, Coulter, *History of Kentucky*, 310.

[41] Ibid

[42] Breen, *The Land Shall be Deluged in Blood: A New History of the Nat Turner Revolt*, 156.

[43] Connelley, Coulter, *History of Kentucky*, 310.

[44] James B. Taylor, *Virginia Baptist Ministers* (Philadelphia, Pennsylvania: J. B. Lippiincott & Co.,1859), 166; digital images, *Google Books* (http://www.books.google.com: accessed 31 January 2019).

[45] Connelley, Coulter, *History of Kentucky*, 310.

[46] Frank L. MvVey, *The Gates Open Slowly: A History of Education in Kentucky* (Lexington, Kentucky: University of Kentucky Press, 1949), 30; digital images, *Google Books* (http://www.books.google.com: accessed 31 January 2019).

[47] Frank L. MvVey, *The Gates Open Slowly: A History of Education in Kentucky* (Lexington, Kentucky: University of Kentucky Press, 1949), 29-30; digital

David was responsible for teaching many children how to read and write. Always the idealist, he established a set of rules designed to shape the children he taught into responsible young adults. From inspiring students to use the terms *"sir & madam"* to punishing those that *"Provoke[d] others during the Hours of Exercise,"*[48] David was committed to instructing his students to behave appropriately.

This period of peace and productivity was short-lived, however, and he once again became the object of religious persecution. This time, it was from within the Baptist Church. After being kicked out of the North District Baptist Association,[49] he made an unprecedented impact on the history of Kentucky.

Assembling other Baptist ministers who similarly protested the slave trade, he helped form the Licking-Locust Association, Friends to Humanity.[50] Founded by thirty-one Baptists, only those who rejected *"perpetual slavery"* could join.[51] The only exception was purchasing slaves *"to liberate them."*[52] This organization did not last long, however, and it was soon disbanded.

David's most significant achievement came shortly after in 1808 when he helped establish the Kentucky Abolition Society. While the Licking-Locust Association was the first anti-slavery

---

images, *Google Books* (http://www.books.google.com: accessed 31 January 2019).

[48] Frank L. MvVey, *The Gates Open Slowly: A History of Education in Kentucky* (Lexington, Kentucky: University of Kentucky Press, 1949), 31; digital images, *Google Books* (http://www.books.google.com: accessed 31 January 2019).

[49] William Elsey Connelley, E. M. Coulter, Ph. D., *History of Kentucky* (Chicago and New York: The American Historical Society, 1992), 311; digital image, *Google Books* (http://www.books.google.com: accessed 1 February 2019).

[50] B.B. Edwards, S. H. Riddel, *American Quarterly Register: Vol. XIV* (Boston, Massachusetts: Press of T. R. Marvin, 1842), 50; digital images, *Google Books* (http://www.books.google.com: accessed 1 February 2019).

[51] Edwards, Riddle, *American Quarterly Register: Vol. XIV*, 50.

[52] Ibid

organization in the United States,[53] it only lasted a short time. In comparison, as President of the Kentucky Abolition Society, David had a lasting and significant effect on the state.

Dedicated to achieving a *"constitutional abolition of slavery and the domestic slave trade,"*[54] the society challenged Kentucky's culture and its economy. Acknowledging that gradual emancipation was the preferred approach, David and his colleagues supported a variety of policies. Vowing to denounce slavery in public, *"ameliorate[ing] the conditions of slaves,"*[55] and promote the rights of freedmen, they constituted an essential part of the counter-culture in Kentucky.

David also petitioned the U.S House of Representatives. On 18 October 1815, he addressed a letter to the Speaker of the House proposing the idea of setting aside land for freed slaves as a place of refuge. The response, however, was not what he hoped for and they turned it down. But David did not give up.

On March 20, 1815, he contacted Thomas Jefferson, suggesting a similar idea. Advocating that slaves be *"prepared by instruction and habit for self-government and for honest pursuits of industry and social duty,"*[56] his suggestion was met with resistance. Told by Jefferson that *"it will yield time to temperate & steady pursuit, to the enlargement of the human mind,"*[57] David again faced a setback.

Despite all these obstacles, however, David achieved a great deal. Prior to his death on November 19, 1819, he had convinced a

---

[53] Connelly, *History of Kentucky*, 311.
[54] John E. Kleber, *The Kentucky Encyclopedia* (Lexington, Kentucky: The University of Press of Kentucky, 1992), 489; digital images, Google Books (http://www.books.google.com: accessed 4 February 2019).
[55] Kleber, *The Kentucky Encyclopedia*, 489.
[56] Thomas Jefferson, *Founders Online* (https://www.founders.archives.gov: accessed 4 February 2019), "Thomas Jefferson to David Barrow, 1 May 1815."
[57] Jefferson, *Founders Online*," Thomas Jefferson to David Barrow, 1 May 1815."

surprising number of slaveholders to question slavery. Some even emancipated their slaves. Although significant personalities of American history are often overlooked, the impact of less well-known pioneers such as Rev. David Barrow cannot be overstated.

## Children

The children of Rev. David Barrow and Sarah Gilliam are as follows:

- **Nathaniel Barrow**: Born March 27, 1744, in Brunswick County,[58] Virginia; died September 24, 1816, in Montgomery County, Kentucky.[59] He married Judith Clark.[60]
- **Elizabeth Barrow**: Born April 3, 1766, in Isle of Wright County, Virginia;[61] died April 1817 in Indiana. She married William Woodward.[62]
- **David Gilliam Barrow**: Born February 25, 1778, in Isle of Wright County, Virginia;[63] died November 19, 1783, in Isle of Wright County, Virginia.[64]
- **Jerusha Barrow**: Born April 9, 1779, in Isle of Wright County, Virginia;[65] died November 19, 1783, in Isle of Wright County, Virginia.[66]

---

[58] Plainfield-Guilford Township Public Library, *Barrow PDF*, 5.
[59] Marylin Smith, *Outline Descendant Report for Rev. David C Barrow* (Barrow Family Association of America)
[60] Smith, *Outline Descendant Report for Rev. David C Barrow*.
[61] Plainfield-Guilford Township Public Library, *Barrow PDF*, 5; Smith, *Outline Descendant Report for Rev. David C Barrow*.
[62] Smith, *Outline Descendant Report for Rev. David C Barrow*.
[63] Ibid
[64] Ibid
[65] Ibid

- **Jonathan Barrow**: Born February 24, 1781, in Isle of Wright County, Virginia;[67] died October 5, 1782, in Isle of Wright County, Virginia.[68]
- **Sarah Barrow**: Born February 8, 1785, in Isle of Wright County, Virginia;[69] died 1857, Montgomery County, Kentucky.[70] She married Richard Hulse.[71]
- **Mary Barrow**: Born February 6, 1786, in Isle of Wright County, Virginia;[72] died February 26, 1786, in Isle of Wright County, Virginia.[73]
- **Abraham Barrow**: Born March 24, 1787, in Isle of Wright County, Virginia;[74] died November 23, 1878, in Hendricks County, Indiana.[75] He first married Ruth Tatman,[76] and Nancy C Foster second.[77]
- **William B Barrow**: Born January 2, 1790, in Montgomery County, Kentucky;[78] died July 9,

---

[66] Plainfield-Guilford Township Public Library, *Barrow PDF*, 5; Smith, *Outline Descendant Report for Rev. David C Barrow*.
[67] . Plainfield-Guilford Township Public Library, *Barrow PDF*, 5; Smith, *Outline Descendant Report for Rev. David C Barrow*.
[68] Plainfield-Guilford Township Public Library, *Barrow PDF*, 5; Smith, *Outline Descendant Report for Rev. David C Barrow*.
[69] Plainfield-Guilford Township Public Library, *Barrow PDF*, 5; Smith, *Outline Descendant Report for Rev. David C Barrow*.
[70] Smith, *Outline Descendant Report for Rev. David C Barrow*.
[71] Ibid
[72] Plainfield-Guilford Township Public Library, *Barrow PDF*, 5; Smith, *Outline Descendant Report for Rev. David C Barrow*.
[73] Smith, *Outline Descendant Report for Rev. David C Barrow*.
[74] Plainfield-Guilford Township Public Library, *Barrow PDF*, 5; Smith, *Outline Descendant Report for Rev. David C Barrow*.
[75] Smith, *Outline Descendant Report for Rev. David C Barrow*.
[76] Ibid
[77] Ibid
[78] . Plainfield-Guilford Township Public Library, *Barrow PDF*,5; Smith, *Outline Descendant Report for Rev. David C Barrow*

1870, in Clark County Kentucky.[79] He married Ann Goodwin Marshall.[80]
- **Hinchea Gilliam Barrow**: Born December 25, 1791, in Montgomery County, Virginia;[81] died March 10, 1856, in Clark County, Kentucky.[82] He married Rachel Scholl.[83]
- **Amy Lee Barrow**: Born November 19, 1793, in Montgomery County, Kentucky;[84] died January 5, 1869, in Calloway County, Missouri.[85] She married Samuel McClure.[86]
- **Rev. David Gilliam Barrow**: Born October 10, 1796;[87] died February 4, 1879, in Montgomery County, Kentucky.[88] He married Lucy Fletcher.[89]

**Conclusion**

In an era when the slave trade was commonly accepted, the Rev. David Barrow's views were considered unconventional. From childhood, he watched as slavery become engrained into the American economy. However, after realizing that slavery could not co-exist morally with Christianity, David became an abolitionist. Putting his life at risk, he preached against the slave

---

[79] Smith, *Outline Descendant Report for Rev. David C Barrow*.
[80] Ibid
[81] Plainfield-Guilford Township Public Library, *Barrow PDF*,5; Smith, *Outline Descendant Report for Rev. David C Barrow*.
[82] Smith, *Outline Descendant Report for Rev. David C Barrow*.
[83] Ibid
[84] Plainfield-Guilford Township Public Library, *Barrow PDF*,5; Smith, *Outline Descendant Report for Rev. David C Barrow*.
[85] Smith, *Outline Descendant Report for Rev. David C Barrow*.
[86] Ibid
[87] Plainfield-Guilford Township Public Library, *Barrow PDF*,5; Smith, *Outline Descendant Report for Rev. David C Barrow*.
[88] Smith, *Outline Descendant Report for Rev. David C Barrow*.
[89] Ibid

trade. Moving to Kentucky for ethical and economic reasons, David helped establish the first abolitionist society in the United States. Although he failed to abolish slavery, his efforts did bring about significant reform. It is because of such men and women as David Barrow that the seeds for abolitionism were planted in American society.

- Born October 10, 1753, in Brunswick County, Virginia,[90] he grew up in a farming community where slavery was accepted.
- A member of the Established Church of England, David Barrow also was accustomed to its conversational nature. Required to take an oath of allegiance to British king,[91] he had to swear loyalty to the church-state government of Virginia.
- After witnessing dissenters go to jail or being fined for refusing to take the oath,[92] he began to become disillusioned with the Church of England. However, it wasn't until he realized that other Christian denominations offered a more personal connection to God that he became a religious dissenter.[93]
- At the age of sixteen, he was baptized by Zachariah Thompson, a Baptist minister, at Fountain Creek Church in Brunswick County, Virginia.[94]
- Under the mentorship of Rev. Zachariah Thompson, David Barrow learned about the importance of the Trinity and the *"inspiration and infallibility of the Holy scripture."*[95]

---

[90] North, *The Barrow Family of Virginia: 1620-1972*,186; University of Kentucky, *Bureau of School Bulletin: 1970-1971*, 19.
[91] University of Wisconsin, *Act of Toleration, May 1689*, 1-2
[92] Davis, Smylie, Thompson, Thompson, Todd, *Virginia Presbyterians in American Life: Hanover Presbytery*, 5.
[93] Samuel Davies, *Sermons on Important* Subjects, V.
[94] University of Kentucky, *Bureau of School Bulletin: 1970-1971*, 19.
[95] Taylor, *Virginia Baptist Ministers*, 167.

- David Barrow's political views also were shaped during this time. Believing in *"the natural equality of man, except in some monstrous cases,"*[96] he condemned slavery as a *"curse."*[97]
- In 1774, David Barrow married Sarah Gillam in Brunswick County, Virginia.[98] He also was ordained as a pastor and invited to become the minister at Mill Swamp Church in Isle of Wright County, Virginia.[99]
- Transforming the local churches into the *"orthodox Churches,"*[100] David was so successful that Mill Swamp Church is where his ministry was *"most favored."*[101]
- Before becoming pastor at Black Creek Church in Southampton County, Virginia in 1778,[102] Rev. David Barrow served in the American Revolution.[103]
- Convincing *"at least three church members to free their slaves,"*[104] he had earned a revered and controversial reputation.
- After being invited to preach at a house in Southampton County in 1778, David Barrow was *"seized by a gang of ruffians"* and *"dragged a mile-*

---

[96] Taylor, *Virginia Baptist Ministers*, 169.
[97] Barrow, *Rev. David Barrow's Journal*.
[98] Plainfield-Guilford Township Public Library, *Barrow PDF*.
[99] Connelley, Coulter, *History of Kentucky*, 310.
[100] Ibid
[101] Taylor, *Virginia Baptist Ministers*, 169.
[102] Breen, *The Land Shall be Deluged in Blood: A New History of the Nat Turner Revolt*, 155.
[103] Connelley, Coulter, *History of Kentucky*, 310.
[104] Breen, *The Land Shall be Deluged in Blood: A New History of the Nat Turner Revolt*, 156.

*half.*"[105] After which, they plunged his head into muddy water twice, and asked *"if he believed."*[106]
- Freeing his slaves in 1784,[107] Rev. David Barrow later moved to Montgomery County, Kentucky in 1798.[108] Preferring to live in a state not as ingrained in slavery, he also wanted to raise his children in this type of environment.
- Becoming pastor at Mount Sterling Church, Goshen, and Lullebegrud Baptist Church,[109] he established the Lullebegrud School for children.[110]
- After being kicked out of the North District Baptist Association for his abolitionist activities,[111] he and thirty-one other Baptists formed the Licking-Locust Association, Friends to Humanity.[112]
- Rev. David Barrow's biggest achievement, however, came in 1808 when he helped establish the Kentucky Abolition Society. Dedicated to achieving a *"constitutional abolition of slavery and the domestic slave trade,"*[113] he believed in the gradual emancipation of slaves.
- On March 20, 1815, David Barrow sent a letter to Thomas Jefferson requesting that slaves be *"prepared by instruction and habit for self-*

---

[105] Connelley, Coulter, *History of Kentucky*, 83.
[106] Connelley, Coulter, *History of Kentucky*, 310.
[107] Breen, *The Land Shall be Deluged in Blood: A New History of the Nat Turner Revolt*, 156.
[108] Connelley, Coulter, *History of Kentucky*, 310.
[109] ibid
[110] MvVey, *The Gates Open Slowly: A History of Education in Kentucky*, 30.
[111] Connelley, Coulter, *History of Kentucky*, 311.
[112] Edwards, Riddle, *American Quarterly Register: Vol. XIV*, 50.
[113] Kleber, *The Kentucky Encyclopedia*, 489

*government and for honest pursuits of industry and social duty.*"[114]
- David even petitioned the U.S. House of Representatives requesting that land be set aside for freed slaves as a place of refuge.
- Rev. David Barrow passed away on November 19, 1819, in Montgomery County, Kentucky.[115]

---

[114] Jefferson, *Founders Online*," Thomas Jefferson to David Barrow, 1 May 1815."
[115] University of Kentucky, *Bureau of School Bulletin: 1970-1971*, 19; Plainfield-Guilford Township Public Library, *Barrow PDF*,5.

# Chapter 4
# John Dickins

From its creation United States has been a beacon for religious and political freedom. After throwing off the shackles of Great Britain, the newly-established government was entrusted with rebuilding society. With a divided community and failing economy, there was much to address. However, the American Revolution also had weakened the ecclesiastical system. With the Protestant Episcopal Church, once the center for stability, losing congregations, and with their schools falling into disrepair, the situation was dim.

Rev. John Dickins, a Methodist minister, however, was dedicated to reforming and rebuilding the Episcopal Church. With the newly-formed country's optimism growing, ecclesiastical leaders like John promoted ideals that inspired a new hope. From promoting anti-slavery doctrine to establishing new schools, he attempted to reform colonial society.

**Rev. John Dickins**: Born 1746 in London, England; died 1798 in Philadelphia, Pennsylvania.[1] He married Elizabeth Yancey in Halifax County, North Carolina.[2]

**Life Story:** Slavery in eighteenth-century Virginia has always been a controversial subject. Endorsed by the government and general population, even the Established Church of England

---

[1] Elbert Ross Zaring, *NorthWestern Christian Advocate* (Chicago, Illinois: Northwestern Christian Advocate, 1916), 1043;digital image, *Google Books* (http://www.books.google.com: accessed 29 October 2018).
[2] Zaring, *NorthWestern Christian Advocate*, 1043.

thrived on the trade of human beings. However, by the end of the American Revolution, the British establishment had collapsed. As a result, dissenting societies now had the opportunity to establish their own denominations and address this injustice. One of these churches attempted to end slavery and to rebuild the educational and ecclesiastical institutions of America. Dedicated to abolishing "*the sin of slavery*,"[3] John Dickins and the Methodist Episcopal Church accepted this challenge, even at the risk of great personal harm.

As a youth at Eton College in Windsor, England, John Dickins' schooling prepared him for this occasion. Raised within an institution that taught the "*Nobility and Gentry*,"[4] his education prepared him to be an "*orator and poet*."[5] During his studies of "*Ovid and Virgil*,"[6] he learned the value of reading, writing, public speaking and being loyal to the Crown.

Arriving in Virginia before the start of the American Revolution, his upbringing clashed with the ideals spread by the Patriots. As a boy, John was educated to support the church-state relationship of Great Britain. Endorsed by the government, the Church of England was financially supported by the Crown. As a result, the Church was the only officially recognized denomination in the colony. However, due to political and economic controversies, it had declined.

---

[3] Daniel de Vinné, *The Methodist Episcopal Church and Slavery* (New York, New York: Francis Hart, 1857), 17; digital images, *Google Books* (http://www.books.google.com: accessed 22 October 2018).

[4] Lionel Cust, *A History of Eton College* (London, England: Duckworth & Co, 1899), 139; digital images, *Google Books* (http://www.books.google.com: accessed 23 October 2018).

[5] Martin Lowther Clarke, *Classical Education In Britain: 1500-1900* (Cambridge, England: Cambridge University Press, 1959), 39; digital images, *Google Books* (http://www.books.google.com: accessed 23 October 2018).

[6] Martin Lowther Clarke, *Classical Education In Britain: 1500-1900* (Cambridge, England: Cambridge University Press, 1959), 40; digital images, *Google Books* (http://www.books.google.com: accessed 23 October 2018).

During this time, John witnessed the downfall of traditional English society. Beginning in 1776,[7] with the dissolution of the House of Burgesses in 1776, politics in Virginia had become polarized. Concerned that England was abusing its power, the delegates from the House of Burgesses reassembled to form a separate government. Praised by patriots and mocked by loyalists, this rogue organization helped usher in the American Revolution.

Observing the rise of anti-British sympathies, John Dickens was aware of the growing influence of the rebel Committee of Safeties. Under the authority of the Continental Congress,[8] these provincial governments represented the revolutionaries in each county. With the usurpation of British law, John watched as a new power flourished. Once the center of governance, the Anglican parishes were now in decline.

Once the political and ecclesiastical foundation, the Church of England was the center of power. From attending Anglican worship services to paying tithes, Church officials required that nonconformists participate.[9] However, when the Act of Toleration was passed in 1689, the situation had changed. Although dissenters could take the *"Oaths of Allegiance of Supremacy"* to avoid being penalized,[10] officials in Virginia rarely observed this law. This policy helped lead to the downfall of the Established Church of England.

---

[7] John Pendleton Kennedy, *Journals of the House of Burgesses of Virginia 1773-1776* (Richmond, Virginia: E Waddey Company, 1905), xxiii; digital images, *Google Books* (http://www.books.google.com: accessed 25 October 2018).

[8] Agnes Hunt, *The Provincial Committees of Safety of the American Revolution* (Cleveland, Ohio: Press of Winn & Judson, 1904), 171; digital images, *Google books* (http://www.books.google.com: accessed 26 October 2018).

[9] Archibald John Stephens, *A Practical of the Laws Relating to the Clergy: Volume 1* (London, England: W. Benning and Co., Booksellers, 1848), 460; digital images, *Google Books* (http://www.books.google.com: accessed 26 October 2018.)

[10] Matthew Gutteridge, *A Digest of English History* (London, England: Relfe Brothers, 1884), 23; digital images, *Google Books* (http://www.books.google.com: accessed 26 October 2018).

With the collapse of the Anglican Church, the colony's educational system also suffered. Designed to teach children "*English and Writing*,"[11] it was the primary means of instruction in Virginia. Overseen by teachers preselected by the minister, this system also suppressed religious dissenters.[12] Like the education he received in England, John Dickins knew Virginians were raised to be loyal Anglicans.

John's opinions concerning this scheme are unknown, but by the time of his arrival in Virginia, opposition by nonconformists was common. From Presbyterians from Northern Ireland to the growth of the Baptist denomination, the ecclesiastical community was changing. Rejecting political associations with the Church of England, even traditional economic ties were challenged by religious dissenters. John supported this movement, especially when the spiritual well-being of the people was concerned.

With the Committee of Safeties protecting the counties, providing supplies for the war effort, and "*examined[examinng] and punished[punishing]*" tories,[13] John Dickins became a revolutionary. Unlike the typical patriot, he took a stance on slavery that exposed him to ridicule. Questioning the unethical nature of the human trade, he also condemned how the Anglican Church supported this system. Seen as an instigator, John had earned a controversial reputation.

When John Dickins became part of the Methodist movement in 1776, he realized how deeply the Church of England was wounded. Led by Rev. John Wesley, an Anglican minister, John

---

[11] William Arthur Maddox, *The Free School idea in Virginia Before the Civil War* (New York, New York: Teacher's College, Columbia University,1918) 105; digital images, *Google Books* (http://www.books.google.com: accessed 27 October 2018).

[12] Arthur Maddox, *The Free School idea in Virginia Before the Civil War*, 105.

[13] Agnes Hunt, *The Provincial Committees of Safety of the American Revolution* (Cleveland, Ohio: Press of Winn & Judson, 1904), 94; digital images, *Google books* (http://www.books.google.com: accessed 27 October 2018).

Dickins believed the Church of England could still be reformed. As he preached to a congregation of *"four or five hundred"* on June 16, 1776,[14] he recognized the irony of the situation. Although an Anglican in name, what he taught was contrary to the tradition of the Church.

Focused on saving the Church of England, he wanted to breathe new life into the age-old establishment. From the beginning, this Christian denomination demanded absolute loyalty to the King. Lacking an emphasis on the *"personal experience"* in Christian life,[15] the spiritual appeal to the Anglicans had been replaced with policy. For those seeking spiritual enlightenment, they learned dissenters and Methodists offered this opportunity.

With the Church's mission to combat the popularity of religious dissension, it is not surprising that the poor were sometimes overlooked.[16] Concerned about this negligence, John Dickins and his fellow Methodists spoke out.

As an itinerant minister, John Dickins knew this wasn't the only reason the church was losing members. On his travels through the backcountry of Virginia, he witnessed the deplorable state of the parishes. From churches in disrepair to ministers that lived in poverty, he witnessed the consequences of the Act of 1776 that weakened the Anglican Church.

Once able to support themselves, the parishes were no longer were financed by the government. Forced to make a living by farming, the salaries of ministers were cut off.[17] Even the required tithes to

---

[14] John Atkinson, *Centennial History of America Methodism* (New York: Cranston & Stowe, 1884), 308; digital images *Google Books* (http://www.books.google.com: accessed 27 October 2018).

[15] Richard P. Heitzenrater, *Wesley and the People Called Methodist: 2$^{nd}$ Edition* (Nashville, Tennessee: Abingdon Press, 2013), 1; digital images, *Google Books* (http://books.google.com: accessed 28 October 2018).

[16] Heitzenrater, *Wesley and the People Called Methodist: 2$^{nd}$ Edition*, 1.

[17] Virginia State Library, Archive Division, *Separation of Church and State in Virginia: A Study in the Development of the Revolution* (Richmond, Virginia:

the Church of England were eliminated.[18] While dissenters rejoiced, an exodus of Anglican ministers moving back to Great Britain was the result. Even Methodists, who were loyalists, left Virginia.

During this turbulent time, the Rev. John Dickins became known as an inspirational preacher. Riding on horseback from community to community, he preached to crowds that flocked to hear his sermons. Educating others about this spiritual illumination, people *"began to praise God"* as they *"roared aloud for mercy."*[19] Holding long meetings, one even lasted *"from twelve at noon to twelve at night, during which God raised up about fifteen more witnesses."*[20]

John Dickins's journeys, however, were not without tribulations. His role as an itinerant minister often led him into life-threatening situations. When he preached, he encountered neighborhoods where his message was rejected. In other cases, he was seen as an Anglican interloper.

In Virginia and North Carolina, he preached that *"slavery is contrary to the laws of God, man and nature, and hurtful to society."*[21] Challenging the livelihood of slaveowners, he recognized that he was putting himself in harm's way. Like his colleague, Bishop Thomas Coke, who was almost attacked by a

---

Virginia State Library, 1910), 45; digital images, *Google Books* (http://www.books.google.com: accessed 28 October 2018).

[18] Virginia State Library, Archive Division, *Separation of Church and State in Virginia: A Study in the Development of the Revolution*, 45.

[19] John Atkinson, *Centennial History of America Methodism* (New York: Cranston & Stowe, 1884), 309; digital images *Google Books* (http://www.books.google.com: accessed 28 October 2018).

[20] Atkinson, *Centennial History of America Methodism*, 309.

[21] Daniel de Vinné, *The Methodist Episcopal Church and Slavery* (New York, New York: Francis Hart, 1857), 15; digital images, *Google Books* (http://www.books.google.com: accessed 29 October 2018).

"*mob*" with "*flaves and clubs*,"[22] John remained dedicated to the abolitionist movement.

Known as a "*Latin and Greek scholar with some knowledge of Hebrew*,"[23] his emphasis on teaching the poor and enslaved was well-known. Advised by Thomas Coke to meet with slaves by "*candle-light*,"[24] he secretly taught the gospel to slaves.

One of the few Methodist circuit riders remaining in the New World, John Dickins witnessed the deterioration of society. With neighborhoods being torn apart, families had to decide where their loyalties lay. From Patriots to Loyalists, politics and religion became heated. With little incentive to unite the country, Rev. John Dickins tried to help ease these tensions. Appointed a circuit rider in 1778, 1779, and 1780 by the Methodist Episcopal Church,[25] he continued to preach about civil rights, and the revival of the Christian spirit. However, it wasn't until the end of the American Revolution that he achieved one of his greatest accomplishments.

During the war, the education system established by the Church of England had writhed. Once the center for receiving an education, educators were instrumental in giving children a basic education. On December 9, 1783, John Dickins is recorded as rebuilding this system. As one of the contributors to the Cokesbury School in

---

[22] Rev. Thomas Coke, *Journals of the Rev. Thomas Coke's Five Visits to America* (London, England: G. Paramore, North, 1793), 35-36.
[23] James E. Kirby, James Kirby, Russel E. Richy, Kenneth E. Rowe, *The Methodists* (Westport, Connecticut, London: Greenwood Press, 1996), 290; digital images, *Google Books* (http://www.books.google.com: accessed 29 October, 2018).
[24] Rev. Thomas Coke, *Journals of the Rev. Thomas Coke's Five Visits to America* (London, England: G. Paramore, North, 1793), 18.
[25] Zaring, *NorthWestern Christian Advocate*, 1043.

North Carolina,[26] he helped establish a *"high school, or preparatory school."*[27]

Providing a Christian education, it mirrored the curriculum of the Anglican schools, but there were fundamental differences. Instead of teaching children to be loyal to Great Britain, the lessons reflected the values of the United States. Unlike the Church of England, teachers taught the principles of the Methodist movement. From promoting civil rights, seeking personal enlightenment, and other Wesleyan traditions, it was considered groundbreaking.

By now, the differences between the Church of England and the Methodists were noticeable. Renamed the Protestant Episcopal Church in 1784 by the General Assembly, the link with Great Britain was abolished.[28] While the traditional Anglican churches were weakened by the political, economic, and ecclesiastical scars of the war, the Methodists had been gaining popularity and stability. Although the Anglicans and Methodists shared spiritual and historical origins, they no longer supported each other. Even the Rev. John Dickins was *"opposed to our [their] continuance in union with the Episcopal Church."*[29] Shortly after in 1785, the Methodist Episcopal Church was founded.[30]

---

[26] The Trinity College Historical Society and the North Carolina Conference Historical Society, *Historic Papers* (North Carolina: The Trinity College Historical, 1912), 23; digital images, *Google Books* (http://www.books.google.com: accessed 29 October 2018); John Atkinson, *Centennial History of America Methodism* (New York: Cranston & Stowe, 1884), 331; digital images *Google Books* (http://www.books.google.com: accessed 27 October 2018).

[27] The Trinity College Historical Society, Historic Papers, 23.

[28] Virginia State Library, Archive Division, *Separation of Church and State in Virginia: A Study in the Development of the Revolution* (Richmond, Virginia: Virginia State Library, 1910), 143; digital images, *Google Books* (http://www.books.google.com: accessed 29 October 2018).

[29] Rev. Francis Asbury, *Journal of the Rev. Francis Asbury: Bishop of the Methodist Episcopal Church: Volume 1* (New York: Lane & Scott, 1852), 366;

Forever separating themselves from the Protestant Episcopal Church, this proved crucial for the development of the United States. Supported by the Rev. John Wesley, John Dickins agreed a schism was appropriate. Stating that *"The English Government has no authority over them [the Methodists], either civil or ecclesiastical, any more than over the states of Holland "*[31] he realized the culture of America had changed. Also, aware that the newly-established denomination lacked official bishops, he gave permission to implement such a system. Naming Rev. Thomas Coke and Rev. Francis Asbury superintendents, the church was now authorized to ordain ministers.[32]

Appointed a deacon at the now famous Christmas Conference of 1784,[33] Rev. John Dickins was essential to the formation of the Methodist Episcopal Church. An associate of Reverend. Coke and Reverend Asbury, he was one of the foremost Methodist ministers

---

digital images, *Google Books* (http://www.books.google.com: accessed 29 October 2018).

[30] Methodist Episcopal Church, *Minutes of the Annual Conference of the Method Episcopal Church for the Years 1773-1828: Volume 1* (New York: T. Mason and G. Lane, 1840), 21; digital books, *Google Books* (http://www.books.google.com: accessed 29 October 2018).

[31] Methodist Episcopal Church, *Minutes of the Annual Conference of the Method Episcopal Church for the Years 1773- 1828: Volume 1* (New York: T. Mason and G. Lane, 1840), 22; digital books, *Google Books* (http://www.books.google.com: accessed 29 October 2018).

[32] Methodist Episcopal Church, *Minutes of the Annual Conference of the Method Episcopal Church for the Years 1773-1828: Volume 1*, 22.

[33] Methodist Episcopal Church, *Minutes of the Annual Conference of the Method Episcopal Church for the Years 1773-1828: Volume 1*, 22.

in Virginia. Responsible for the naming of the denomination,[34] John was also the first to be informed about this plan.[35]

When the Methodist Episcopal Church Conference met in 1789, John Dickin's career took an unexpected turn. As the Methodist communities continued to grow, the number of itinerant ministers also expanded. However, there remained a need to provide "*inexpensive books and pamphlets*" to Christians on the frontier.[36] Appointed Book Steward,[37] he donated $600 of his own money to establish the Book Concern, a Methodist publishing company.[38]

Living in Philadelphia, John Dickins no longer traveled the country. Focused on supporting the mission of the church, he could now publish the values of Methodism on a grand scale. From the abolishment of slavery and hymn-books,[39,40] to how to live in imitation of Christ,[41] all the lessons of John Wesley were shared. Considered innovative at the time, he proved instrumental in expanding the Church. Today known as The United Methodist

---

[34] Joseph Wakeley, *Lost Chapters Recovered from the Early History of American Methodism* (Bedford, Massachusetts: Applewood Books, 1858), 304; digital images, *Google Books* (http://www.books.google.com: accessed 30 October 2018).

[35] Joseph Wakeley, *Lost Chapters Recovered from the Early History of American Methodism* (Bedford, Massachusetts: Applewood Books, 1858), 303; digital images, *Google Books* (http://www.books.google.com: accessed 30 October.

[36] The United Methodist Publishing House, *The United Methodist Publishing House* (https://www.umph.org/: accessed October 30 2018), "History."

[37] Methodist Episcopal Church, *Minutes of the Annual Conference of the Method Episcopal Church for the Years 1773-1828: Volume 1* (New York: T. Mason and G. Lane, 1840), 34; digital books, *Google Books* (http://www.books.google.com: accessed 30 October 2018).

[38] Methodist Episcopal Church, *Minutes of the Annual Conference of the Method Episcopal Church for the Years 1773-1828: Volume 1*, "History."

[39] John H. Wigger, *Methodism and the Rise of Popular Christianity in American* (Urbana and Chicago: University of Illinois Press, 1998), 256; digital images, *Google Books* (http://www.books.google.com: accessed 30 October 2018).

[40] Wigger, *Methodism and the Rise of Popular Christianity in American*, 256.

[41] Ibid

Publishing House, it is one of the most influential denominational publishing houses.

Passing away on September 27, 1798, the Rev. John Dickins lived an eventful life. Seen as *"one of the greatest characters that ever graced the pulpit or adorned the society of ministers or Methodists,"*[42] he proved crucial to the success of the Methodist movement. Chiseled into his gravestone are these parting words: *"Here lieth who he, in the case of God, never feared or flattered man."*[43] Afraid only of God, without his contributions, the United States would have turned out differently.

## Conclusion

The reconstruction of the United States after the American Revolution was a difficult time for Virginians. With a weakened economy, ruined educational system, and the collapse of the Church of England, everyone struggled. With neighborhoods divided between Patriots and Loyalists, even politics became polarized. However, a new denomination arose that gave birth to a renaissance of hope.

The Rev. John Dickins, a minister from the Methodist Episcopal Church, was a creator of this revival. Born in London, England, he immigrated to Virginia before the War for Independence. A witness to the decline of the Church of England, he experienced the political and ecclesiastical consequences. Once the spiritual and political authority in each county, the parishes were known to

---

[42] Joseph Wakeley, *Lost Chapters Recovered from the Early History of American Methodism* (Bedford, Massachusetts: Applewood Books, 1858), 506; digital images, *Google Books* (http://www.books.google.com: accessed 30 October 2018).

[43] Wakeley, *Lost Chapters Recovered from the Early History of American Methodism*, 506.

support the British government. But, by 1776, the Anglican communities began to suffer.

Abolishing government funding to the Church of England, the Act of 1776 removed the punishments imposed on nonconformists. With the revolutionaries in charge of the colony, John Dickins had mixed emotions. As part of the Methodist movement within the Anglican Church, he was trying to reform the organization.

In 1784, in obedience to values of the new American government, the Church of England was renamed to the Protestant Episcopal Church. One year later, the Methodist formed their own denomination, the Methodist Episcopal Church. With his allegiance to Great Britain dissolved, Rev. John Dickins continued to build on his labors.

A critic of slavery, he disapproved of how the United States' economy was based on the trade of human beings. He was also an outspoken opponent of the Church of England for using slavery as a means of funding. Risking life and limb, he became known for promoting anti-slavery ideals.

An advocate for receiving an education, he also attempted to create a new school system for children. Seeing a need to unite the country, John helped found a Christian high school in North Carolina. While reading and writing were taught, the principles of Methodism were presented as well. From a need for spiritual enlightenment to educating others on civil rights, the teachings of John Wesley were included.

By the end of his career, he was designated as the editor of the Book Concern, a Methodist publishing company. Able to circulate educational material for the church, John Dickins influenced the United States on a grand scale. Reforming how Americans viewed slavery, education, and religion, he assisted greatly in building the America we know today.

- Born in London, England, in 1746,[44] John Dickins was raised in an Anglican household.
- As a student at Eton College in Windsor, England, John was taught the values of the *"Nobility and Gentry."*[45]
- With the dissolution of the House of Burgesses in 1776,[46] he witnessed the collapse of British rule.
- Joining the Methodist movement in the Church of England in 1776,[47] John Dickins became an itinerant minister. Dedicated to reforming the Anglican Church, he preached on the importance of a having a *"personal experience"* with Christ.[48]
- Speaking before the poor and disfranchised, John realized the Church of England was being negligent.
- When the Act of 1776 was passed, the salaries of Anglican ministers were cut off for a year.[49] Now forced to make a living by farming, those loyal to England left for Great Britain, resigned, or changed careers.
- During this time, he witnessed the political and religious division within Virginia. Now controlled by local Committee of Safeties, each county was governed by the Patriots. Those who were a threat were brought being the committees to be judged.
- Preaching that *"slavery is contrary to the laws of God, man and nature, and hurtful to society,"*[50] he often participated in dangerous situations.[51]

---

[44] Zaring, *NorthWestern Christian Advocate*, 1043.
[45] Cust, *A History of Eton College*, 139.
[46] Kennedy, *Journals of the House of Burgesses of Virginia 1773-1776*, xxiii.
[47] Atkinson, *Centennial History of America Methodism*, 308.
[48] Heitzenrater, *Wesley and the People Called Methodist: 2nd Edition*, 1.
[49] Virginia State Library, Archive Division, *Separation of Church and State in Virginia: A Study in the Development of the Revolution*, 45.
[50] de Vinné, *The Methodist Episcopal Church and Slavery*, 15.

- In order to recreate a school system for children, he contributed to the Cokesbury School in North Carolina,[52] establishing the first Methodist *"high school."*[53]
- In 1785, one year after the Church of England was reorganized as the Protestant Episcopal Church,[54] John Dickins was *"opposed"* to a *"continuance in union with the Episcopal Church"*[55] By this time, the two denominations no longer supported each other.
- A devout follower of Rev. John Wesley, the leader of the Methodist movement, John believed that *"The English Government has no authority over them [the Methodists], either civil or ecclesiastical, any more than over the states of Holland."*[56]
- As one of the foremost Methodist ministers, John was responsible for the naming of the denomination.[57]
- Appointed Book Steward of the Book Concern in 1789, he was responsible for providing *"inexpensive books and pamphlets"* to itinerant ministers.[58]

---

[51] Coke, *Journals of the Rev. Thomas Coke's Five Visits to America*, 35-36.

[52] The Trinity College Historical Society and the North Carolina Conference Historical Society, *Historic Papers*, 23; Atkinson, *Centennial History of America Methodism*, 331.

[53] The Trinity College Historical Society, Historic Papers, 23.

[54] Virginia State Library, Archive Division, *Separation of Church and State in Virginia: A Study in the Development of the Revolution*, 143.

[55] Asbury, *Journal of the Rev. Francis Asbury: Bishop of the Methodist Episcopal Church: Volume 1*, 366.

[56] Methodist Episcopal Church, *Minutes of the Annual Conference of the Method Episcopal Church for the Years 1773-1828: Volume 1*, 22.

[57] Wakeley, *Lost Chapters Recovered from the Early History of American Methodism*, 304.

[58] The United Methodist Publishing House, *The United Methodist Publishing House*, "History."

- Passing on September 27, 1798, he was viewed as *"one of the greatest characters that ever graced the pulpit or adorned the society of ministers or Methodists."*[59]

---

[59] Wakeley, *Lost Chapters Recovered from the Early History of American Methodism*, 506.

# Chapter 5
# Sarah Winston Syme Henry

Among the less-known aspects of colonial Virginia are the lives of women. Living in a restricted society where men held political and economic power, women were at a disadvantage. Expected to perform specific duties, women's "*sole preserve*" was centered on "*marriage and motherhood*".[1] However, not every woman was inhibited by these limitations. Despite this tradition, it was not uncommon for women occasionally to break from these norms.

The life and ventures of Sarah Winston is such an example. Born into an influential family, she was accustomed to the finer things in life. Although during her childhood, she learned that she would have to fulfill certain duties; however, she was not a typical eighteenth-century woman. Breaking with tradition, she raised her children outside of the Church of England and taught them lessons deemed inappropriate by the Anglican Church. One result was that one of her sons, Patrick Henry, was inspired to become one of the leaders of the American Revolution.

**Sarah Winston**: Birth date unknown; died November 1781 in Amherst County, Virginia.[2]

---

[1] Linda E. Speth, Alison Duncan Hirsch, *Women, Family, and Community in Colonial America: Two Perspectives* (1983; reprint, New York, New York: Routledge, 2011), 7; digital images, *Google Books* (http://www.books.google.com: 15 January 2018).
[2] Find a Grave.* *Find a Grave*, database with images (http://www.findagrave.com: accessed 15 January 2018), memorial 31363931, Sarah Winston Henry (death 1781), Winton Plantation, Clifford, Amherst County, Virginia; gravestone photograph by Eric Atkisson.

**Sarah Winston's Parentage**: Isaac Winston, an immigrant from Wales,[3] and Mary Dabney.[4]

**Life Story**: Women in colonial Virginia were often at a disadvantage, both socially and economically. Seen as second-class citizens, the privileges and finances of women were also limited. The daughter of a wealthy settler, Sarah Winston was expected to obey the social norms placed on her; however, such restrictions would not last.

In her childhood, she was taught that women were supposed to take on passive roles. Learning by the example of her mother, she was educated on how to manage household chores. From taking care of children to learning how to cook, her duties were limited to home and family. Nor did she receive a high-level of education.[5] Despite these constraints, however, Sarah forged her own path

As a subordinate to her father, Sarah Winston became accustomed to following the norms of her culture. While women were limited to household duties; men received a higher education, took part in government, owned property, and served their community.[6] Women who broke this order *"faced public ridicule, and occasional legal admonishment for their actions."*[7]

When Sarah became old enough to marry, the freedoms she enjoyed, according to English society, would not last. Raised from

---

[3] William Henry, *Henry Genealogy: The Descendants of Samuel Henry and Lurana (Cady) Henry* (Press of T.R. Marvin and Son: Boston, Massachusetts, 1915), 199; digital images, *Google Books* (http://www.books.google.com: 15 January 2018).

[4] Henry, *Henry Genealogy: The Descendants of Samuel Henry and Lurana (Cady) Henry*, 199.

[5] Gettysburg College, *Gettysburg College* (http://public.gettysburg.edu/~tshannon/341/sites/Gender%20and%20Sexuality/Gender%20Roles.htm: accessed 19 January 2018), "Gender Roles in Colonial America."

[6] Gettysburg College, *Gettysburg College*, "Gender Roles in Colonial America."

[7] Ibid

childhood to become a mother, women did not usually remain unmarried. It was unacceptable for women to remain single.

As an unwed woman, Sarah Winston had the ability to own personal property and real property."[8] As a result, she controlled her finances, could sell her land, or give it to someone else. She also could enter into contracts.[9] Free to acquire indentured servants and slaves, she could participate in English society. This power even allowed her to sue her debators.[10]

Unfortunately, this situation was short-lived. After Sarah's first marriage to John Syme,[11] a prosperous settler, all these liberties disappeared. No longer could she own land, nor could she control her finances.[12, 13] As a wife, her property, including her personal possessions, belonged to her husband. She even had to get permission to *"enter into a contract, execute a deed, or make a will."*[14]

Like her father, Isaac Winston, her husband, John Syme, also was a prominent landowner. Beginning on July 19, 1724, he purchased 4,600 acres of land in Hanover County.[15] By August 25, 1731, he

---

[8] Linda E. Speth, Alison Duncan Hirsch, *Women, Family, and Community in Colonial America: Two Perspectives* (1983; reprint, New York, New York: Routledge, 2011), 8; digital images, *Google Books* (http://www.books.google.com: 20 January 2018).

[9] Linda E. Speth, Alison Duncan Hirsch, *Women, Family, and Community in Colonial America: Two Perspectives*, 8.

[10] Ibid

[11] Norine Campbell Gregory, *Some Ancient landowners in Saint Martin's Parish, Hanover County, Virginia* (Hanover County, Virginia: New Papyrus Co., Inc, 2001), 241.

[12] Linda E. Speth, Alison Duncan Hirsch, *Women, Family, and Community in Colonial America: Two Perspectives*, 8.

[13] Ibid

[14] Ibid

[15] Online Catalog: Images & indexes," database with images, *The Library of Virginia* (http://lva1.hosted.exlibrisgroup.com: accessed 20 January 2018), John Syme, 19 July 1724, 4600 acres, Virginia, Colonial Land Office, Patents, 1623-1774; Library of Virginia.

had been granted 26, 199 acres of land.[16] However, unlike Isaac, John political power directly influenced Sarah's role in society.

The wife of a vestryman in St. Paul's Parish in Hanover County, Virginia, Sarah lived by the social norms of the Church of England.[17] As John Syme was expected to act as an *"authority in all the weightier matters of the Parish,"*[18] she had to faithfully attend church, educate her children, and support her husband. Sarah Winston Syme also encouraged her husband in politics. From 1720 to 1722, John Syme was a member of the House of Burgesses, the legislative body in Virginia.[19] However, after John's death around 1732,[20] her role changed drastically.

During this time, Sarah Winston Syme married John Henry, an immigrant from Aberdeen, Scotland.[21] Like herself, he had an inclination and a desire to help society prosper. The differences

---

[16] "Online Catalog: Images & indexes," database with images, *The Library of Virginia* (http://lva1.hosted.exlibrisgroup.com: accessed 20 January 2018), John Syme, 19 July 1724, 4600 acres; 17 August 1725, 400 acres; 24 February 1729, 400 acres; 28 September 1730, 3400 acres; 28 September 1730, 5820 acres; 28 September 28 1730, 5629 acres, 25 August 1731, 1900 acres; 25 August 1731, 4050 acres, Virginia, Colonial Land Office, Patents, 1623-1774; Library of Virginia.

[17] C. G. Chamberlayne, *The Vestry Book of Saint Paul's Parish* (1940; reprint, Richmond, Virginia: Virginia State Library and Archives, 1989), 126.

[18] John Steer, *Parish Law, being a digest of the law relating to parishes, churches, parish registers, ministers, etc* (London, England: Saunders and Benning, Law Booksellers, 1843), 273; digital images, *Google Books* (http://www.books.google.com: accessed 21 October 2018).

[19] H. R. Mcilwaine, *Journals of the House of Burgesses of Virginia: 1712-1714, 1715, 1718, 1720-1722, 1732-1726* (Richmond, Virginia: Virginia General Assembly, 1912), 16; digital images, *Internet Archive* (https://archive.org: accessed 21 October 2018).

[20] John Kukla, *Patrick Henry: Champion of Liberty* (New York, New York: Simon and Schuster, 2017); digital images, *Google Books* (http://www.books.google.com: accessed 21 October 2018).

[21] Dr. Robert Alonzo Brock, *Virginia and Virginians* (Richmond, Virginia: H. H. Hardesty, Publisher, 1888), 66; digital images, *Google Books* (http://www.books.google.com: accessed 21 October 2018).

between her first and second marriages, however, were not limited to the degree to which husband and wife shared similar interests.

Despite her second-class status, they shared the viewpoint that she deserved more freedom. Like John Syme, John Henry was also elected a vestryman; but unlike John Syme, John Henry was an influential businessman.[22] Perhaps, it was his influence in political affairs that allowed Sarah to create her own destiny. But, whatever the reason, her influence had a great impact on her community.

She had been taught that Virginia wasn't an easy place in which to live. Raised within a Presbyterian household, she was taught to distrust the Church of England. As an adult, she became aware of the penalties of not attending Anglican church services.

As one of the few English colonies that embraced the Church of England as the official religion, Virginia's government and church were one entity. Those Christians that dissented from the Anglican Church were *"called before the court and fined."*[23] Protected by the Act of Toleration of 1689, nonconformists could take an oath of allegiance to the Crown to be granted religious tolerance.[24] However, Virginia officials often dismissed this law and still fined Presbyterians, Quakers, and Baptists that legally attended services at their preapproved meeting houses.[25]

---

[22] Eugenia G. Glazebrook, Preston G. Glazebrook, *Virginia Migration: Hanover County* (1943; reprint, Baltimore, Maryland: Genealogical Publishing Company, Inc, 2002), 55-56.

[23] Robert P. Davis, James H. Smylie, Dean K. Thompson, Ernest Trice Thompson, William Newton Todd, *Virginia Presbyterians in American Life: Hanover Presbytery (1755-1980)* (Richmond, Virginia: Hanover Presbytery, 1982), 19.

[24] Thomas S. Kidd, *Encyclopedia Virginia* (https://www.encyclopediavirginia.org: accessed 22 January 2018), "Act of Toleration 1689."

[25] Robert P. Davis, James H. Smylie, Dean K. Thompson, Ernest Trice Thompson, William Newton Todd, *Virginia Presbyterians in American Life: Hanover Presbytery (1755-1980)* (Richmond, Virginia: Hanover Presbytery, 1982), 27.

Ironically, Sarah didn't know how her upbringing would so dramatically affect Virginia history. After the birth of her second son, Patrick Henry, on May 29, 1736,[26] she became more involved with the Presbyterian community. A devoted follower of the Presbyterian minister, Samuel Davies, she took young Patrick to hear Rev. Davies' sermons in Hanover County.[27]

An inspirational speaker, it is not surprising that Sarah Winston Syme Henry and other dissenters preferred his sermons. By now, the Church of England was losing its congregations due to the energetic nonconformist message of Rev. Davies.

Breaking from the Anglican Church, Sarah surpassed the gender role imposed on her by attending Presbyterian worship services. Supported by her husband, John Henry, Sarah continued to worship as a Presbyterian despite the criticisms leveled against her. Heartened by the proclamation of Samuel Davies that *"liberty, our property, our lives, and our religion,"*[28] were *"no longer ensured to us with the usual firmness of the British constitution,"*[29] she was encouraged to endure these hardships.

The enthusiasm expressed in personal salvation was another belief Sarah Winston Syme Henry embraced. Expressing a *"spontaneous and expressive"* interest in the glory of God's grace,[30] she was

---

[26] Patrick Henry Memorial Foundation, *Patrick Henry Memorial Foundation Red Hill* (http://www.redhill.org: accessed 23 January 2016), "Henry's Early Life and Times."

[27] David J. Vaughan, *Give me Liberty, The Uncompromising Statesmanship of Patrick Henry* (Nashville, Tennessee: Cumberland House, 1997), 31; digital images, *Google Books* (http://books.google.com: accessed 23 January 2018); Massachusetts Sabbath School Society, *Memoir of the Rev. Samuel Davies* (Boston, Massachusetts: Massachusetts Sabbath School Union, 1832), 77.

[28] Samuel Davies, *Sermons on Important Subjects* (1810; reprint, London, England: Forgotten Books, 2012), 36.

[29] Samuel Davies, *Sermons on Important Subjects*, 36.

[30] Philp N. Mulder, *A Controversial Spirit: Evangelical Awakenings in the South* (New York, New York: Oxford University Press, 2002), 19; digital images, *Google Books* (http://www.books.google.com: accessed 23 January 2018).

looked down upon by members of the declining Church of England.

Her participation in the communion of the Presbyterian Church was also unpopular with her Anglican neighbors. Preferring to sit with the congregation during this sacrament, she rejected the traditions of the Church of England.[31] Based on the model of the Scottish Presbyterian Church, communicants sat as an act of defiance. Historically, members of the Scottish Church were forced to kneel during the Lord's Supper, and her fellow Presbyterians had brought this tradition from Scotland.

Sarah Winston Syme Henry also embraced another ideal of Davies: the education of the African and African-American slaves. Davies described this commitment when he stated *"these poor unhappy Africans are objects of my compassion, and I think the most proper objects of the society's charity."*[32] One can envision Sarah attending worship services at the Hanover Meeting House as three hundred Africans flocked to hear Reverend Davies preach.[33] And Presbyterians believed in other doctrines that angered the establishment.

Supporting the practice that allowed ministers to be unofficially ordained in *"log cabin"* colleges to meet the demands of a growing frontier,[34] Sarah was seen as a controversial figure.

Because of her support for the dissenters of Hanover County, she exerted great influence upon the future of the Virginia Colony. Under her guidance, her son, Patrick grew up to be a revolutionary, and would become one of the Founding Fathers of

---

[31] Philp N. Mulder, *A Controversial Spirit: Evangelical Awakenings in the South* (New York, New York: Oxford University Press, 2002), 18; digital images, *Google Books* (http://www.books.google.com: accessed 23 January 2018).
[32] Massachusetts Sabbath School Society, *Memoir of the Rev. Samuel Davies* (Boston, Massachusetts: Massachusetts Sabbath School Union, 1832), 25.
[33] Massachusetts Sabbath School Society, *Memoir of the Rev. Samuel Davies*, 25.
[34] Dr. Robert Alonzo Brock, *Virginia and Virginians*, 66.

the United States.[35] One of her daughters would even marry a cousin of James Madison, another Founding Father.[36]

Despite breaking from the role imposed upon her, Sarah also had a conflictive relationship with John Henry. Never wavering from the Church of England, John's unbending loyalty to the established church often strained their relationship. Raised in a household that was sympathetic to religious dissenters, Sarah's father was *"fined for permitting Presbyterians to worship on his property without a licensed meeting house."*[37] By contrast, John Henry attended St. Paul's Parish where a brother, also named Patrick Henry, was the presiding minster.[38] Convinced that Rev Davies *"had seduc'd some unwary people,"*[39] he believed that the New-Light Presbyterians, like Sarah, were driven into the *"heights of religious phrenzy."*[40]

Sarah Winston Syme Henry and John Henry had a total of nine children. Beginning with William Henry born in 1734, who

---

[35] Gaston Espinosa, *Religion and the American Presidency* (Chichester : New York: Columbia University Press, 2009), 114-115; digital images, *Google Books* (http://www.books.google.com: accessed 25 January 2018).

[36] Find a Grave.* *Find a Grave*, database with images (http://www.findagrave.com: accessed 25 January 2018), memorial 83391790, Susannah Henry Madison (death 1831), Smith's Grove, Warren County, Kentucky; gravestone photograph by Bert Higginbotham; Helen R. Prilaman, *A Place Apart: A Brief History of the Early Williamson Road and North Roanoke Valley Presidents and Places* (Baltimore, Maryland: Genealogical Publishing Company, 1997), 70; digital images, *Google Books* (http://www.books.google.com: accessed 25 January 2018)

[37] John A. Ragosta, *Patrick Henry Proclaiming a Revolution* (New York, New York: Taylor and Francis, 2017), 13; digital images, *Google Books* (http://www.books.google.com: accessed 27 January 2018).

[38] C. G. Chamberlayne, *The Vestry Book of Saint Paul's Parish* (1940; reprint, Richmond, Virginia: Virginia State Library and Archives, 1989), 148.

[39] Thomas E. Buckley, *Establishing Religious Freedom: Jefferson's Statute in Virginia* (Charlottesville, Virginia: University of Virginia, 2013), _; digital images, *Google Books* (http://www.books.google.com: accessed 27 January 2018).

[40] Buckley, *Establishing Religious Freedom: Jefferson's Statute in Virginia*, _.

became a lieutenant in the Virginia militia,[41] her liberal influence left its mark upon and inspired all of them. From housewives, soldiers, and politicians, it is because of her persistence that the Henry family became famous.

On her death bed in November 1784 in Amherst County, Virginia,[42] Sarah had lived a full life. Her desire to live as a religious dissenter helped plant the seeds of rebellion for the American Revolution. It is true that Patrick Henry played a significant in this movement, but without the guidance of his mother, Sarah Winston Syme Henry, this would never have occurred.

**Children**

The children of Sarah Winston Syme and John Syme are as follows:

- **John Syme, Jr,** born about 1729;[43] died before December 1796.[44] He married Mildred Meriwether.[45]

---

[41] Find a Grave.* *Find a Grave*, database with images (http://www.findagrave.com: accessed 27 January 2018), memorial, Lieutenant William Henry (death 1784), Winton Plantation, Clifford, Amherst County, Virginia; gravestone photograph by SheWalksTheseHills.

[42] *Find a Grave*, memorial 31363931, Sarah Winston Henry (death 1781), gravestone photograph by Eric Atkisson.

[43] Alexander Brown, *The Cabells and their Kin* (Cambridge, England: The Riverside Press, 1895), 188; digital books, *Google Books* (http://www.books.google.com: accessed 30 January 2018).

[44] Eugenia G. Glazebrook, Preston G. Glazebrook, *Virginia Migration: Hanover County* (1943; reprint, Baltimore, Maryland: Genealogical Publishing Company, Inc, 2002), 72.

[45] Alexander Brown, *The Cabells and their Kin*, 188.

The children of Sarah Winston Syme Henry and John Henry are as follows:

- **William Henry**, born 1734 in Hanover County;[46] died 1784.[47]
- **Patrick Henry**, born May 29, 1736, in Hanover County;[48] died on June 6, 1799.[49] He married (1st) Sarah Shelton and (2nd) Dorothea Spotswood Dandridge.[50]
- **Anne Henry Christian**, died 27 May 1790.[51] She married William Christian.
- **Jane Henry Meredith**, died 1819 in Amherst County, Virginia.[52] She married Samuel Meredith.[53]

---

[46] *Find a Grave*, database, memorial 31364023, Lieutenant William Henry (1734-1784), gravestone photograph by SheWalksTheseHills.

[47] *Find a Grave*, database, memorial 31364023, Lieutenant William Henry (1734-1784), gravestone photograph by SheWalksTheseHills.

[48] Find a Grave.* *Find a Grave*, database with images (http://www.findagrave.com: accessed 30 January 2018), memorial 472, Patrick Henry (29 May 1736-6 June 1799), Henry Cemetery, Charlotte County, Virginia; gravestone photograph by Signers Tour.

[49] *Find a Grave*, memorial 472, Patrick Henry (29 May 1736-6 June 1799), gravestone photograph by Signers Tour.

[50] Find a Grave.* *Find a Grave*, database with images (http://www.findagrave.com: accessed 30 January 2018), memorial 17826837, Dorothea Dandridge (1755-11 February 1831), Henry County, Charlotte County, Virginia; gravestone photograph by Ssuan Lewis Arday; Henry, *Henry Genealogy: The Descendants of Samuel Henry and Lurana (Cady) Henry*, 200.

[51] Find a Grave.* *Find a Grave*, database with images (http://www.findagrave.com: accessed 30 January 2018), memorial 65730429, Anne Henry Christian (Death 27 May 1790),Bullitt Family Cemetery, Louisville, Jefferson County, Kentucky; gravestone photograph by Susan Lewis Arday.

[52] Henry, *Henry Genealogy: The Descendants of Samuel Henry and Lurana (Cady) Henry*, 202; Find a Grave.* *Find a Grave*, database with images (http://www.findagrave.com: accessed 30 January 2018), memorial 69448916, Jane Henry Meredeith (death 1719), Winton Plantation, Clifford, Amherst County, Virginia; gravestone photograph by D. Thompson.

[53] Henry, *Henry Genealogy: The Descendants of Samuel Henry and Lurana (Cady) Henry*, 202; Amherst County, Virginia, *Wills and Probate Records, 1652-*

- **Susannah Henry Madison**, died 1831 in Kentucky.[54] She married Thomas Madison.[55]
- **Elizabeth Henry Campbell Russel**, born 1749 in Hanover County;[56] died 18 March 1825 in Smyth County, Virginia.[57] She married (1st) General William Campbell and (2nd) William Russel.[58]
- **Lucy Henry Valentine**, born in Hanover County. She married Valentine Wood.[59]
- **Mary Henry Bowyer,** born in Hanover County. She married Luke Bowyer.[60]
- **Sarah Henry**, born in Hanover County.[61]

---

*1983: 571, "Samuel Meredith," 6 August 1808; digital images, Ancestry, Ancestry.com (https://search.ancestry.com: accessed 30 January 2018).*

[54] Find a Grave.* *Find a Grave*, database with images (http://www.findagrave.com: accessed 31 January 2018), memorial 83391790, Susannah Henry (Death1831),Smith's Grove Cemetery, Smith's Grove, Warren County, Kentucky; gravestone photograph by Bert Higginbotham.

[55] Henry, *Henry Genealogy: The Descendants of Samuel Henry and Lurana (Cady) Henry*, 200.

[56] Library of Virginia, *Virginia Women In History* (http://www.lva.virginia.gov/: accessed 31 January 2018), "Elizabeth Henry Campbell Russell.

[57] Cynthia A. Kierner, Sandra Gioia Treadway, *Virginia Women: Their Lives and Times, Volume 1* (Athens, Georgia: University of Georgia Press, 2015), 173; digital images, *Google Books* (http://www.books.gooogle.com: accessed 31 January 2018).

[58] Anne Russell Dus Cognets, *William Russel and his Descendants* (Lexington, Kentucky: Samuel F. Wilson, 1884), 15; digital images, *Google Books* (http://www.books.google.com: accessed 31 January 2018).

[59] Dr. Philip Slaughters, *Genealogical and Historical Notes on Culpepper Virginia* (Culpepper, Virginia: Raleigh Travers Green, 1900), 76-77; digital images, *Google Books* (http://www.books.google: accessed 31 January 2018).

[60] Dr. Philip Slaughters, *Genealogical and Historical Notes on Culpepper Virginia*, 67-77.

[61] Ibid

## Conclusion

Life in eighteenth-century Virginia challenged men and women from all levels of society. From the upper-class statesmen to the humble farmer, each faced their own trials. For women, however, their roles were especially restricted. Unlike men, these restrictions prevented women from influencing their community; but not every woman accepted these limitations.

Sarah Winston Syme Henry, one of the most respected women in Hanover County, Virginia, objected to these cultural restrictions. Raised in a household that embraced the Presbyterian denomination, this participation as a religious dissenter forever changed her destiny. Refusing to attend worship services in the Established Church of England, she also rejected the gender role placed on women.

Through her actions, she not only inspired her family's revolutionary tendencies, but helped plant the seeds of the American Revolution. From Patrick Henry's liberal upbringing, to influencing society itself, she had a tremendous impact on the Virginia Colony.

- Born in Hanover County, Virginia, she was the daughter of Isaac Winston[62], a religious dissenter.[63]
- Raised in a household surrounded by controversy, her father was *"fined for permitting Presbyterians to worship on his property without a licensed meeting house.*[64]
- From her youth, she became accustomed to the values that society placed on females. Taught how to raise children and manage a household, she was supposed to act passively.

---

[62] William Henry, *Henry Genealogy: The Descendants of Samuel Henry and Lurana (Cady)*, 15.
[63] Ragosta, *Patrick Henry Proclaiming a Revolution*, 13.
[64] Ibid

- In adulthood, Sarah Winston enjoyed freedoms that married women did not have. As a single woman, she controlled her finances, could own land and could enter into contracts.[65]
- After her first marriage to John Syme all her property and finances belonged to her husband.
- As a housewife, she supported John Syme's role as a vestryman in St. Paul's Parish and as a member of the House of Burgesses.[66]
- Prohibited from participating in politics, Sarah could face *"public ridicule, and occasional legal admonishment for their actions,"*[67] if she achieved political influence.
- During her second marriage to John Henry, a liberally educated Scottish immigrant,[68] more freedoms were given to her. A frequent listener of the sermons of the Presbyterian minister, Samuel Davies,[69] she was seen negatively by her Anglican neighbors.
- Embracing the theology of New-Light Presbyterians, Sarah emphasized a personal salvation and was dedicated to educating Africans about Christianity.[70]

---

[65] Duncan Hirsch, *Women, Family, and Community in Colonial America: Two Perspectives*, 8.

[66] Mcilwaine, *Journals of the House of Burgesses of Virginia: 1712-1714, 1715, 1718, 1720-1722, 1732-1726*, 16; Chamberlayne, *The Vestry Book of Saint Paul's Parish*, 126, 129, 130, 132.

[67] Gettysburg College, *Gettysburg College*, "Gender Roles in Colonial America."

[68] Brock, *Virginia and Virginians*, 66.

[69] Vaughan, *Give Me Liberty, The Uncompromising Statesmanship of Patrick Henry*, 31; Massachusetts Sabbath School Society, *Memoir of the Rev. Samuel Davies*, 77.

[70] Massachusetts Sabbath School Society, *Memoir of the Rev. Samuel Davies*, 25.

- Despite the disapproval of the Anglican minister, Patrick Henry, her brother-in-law,[71] she continued to take her son to hear Rev. Samuel Davies.[72]
- By her death in 1784 in Amherst County, Virginia, she had raised her children to value religious and political freedoms.[73] Patrick Henry, one of the Founding Fathers, was especially inspired by her example.

---

[71] Buckley, *Establishing Religious Freedom: Jefferson's Statute in Virginia*, _.
[72] Massachusetts Sabbath School Society, *Memoir of the Rev. Samuel Davies*, 77.
[73] *Find a Grave*, memorial 31363931, Sarah Winston Henry (death 1781), gravestone photograph by Eric Atkisson.

# Chapter 6
# Thomas Smith

The American Revolution, resulting from political, religious, and social-economical conflict, impacted all levels of colonial society. As the preexisting government collapsed due to the rise of the Committee of Safeties and the shadow Patriot government, the seeds of rebellion were planted. Patriots from all backgrounds became participants in the escalating, anti-British sentiment. Men, poor and rich alike, joined these committees to assist the American cause.

Thomas Smith, a rector of the Church of England in Westmoreland County, Virginia, was such a person. Initially an English Loyalist, he eventually joined the Americans and forever altered the allegiance of his Anglican parish.

**Thomas Smith**: Born 1739 in King and Queen County, Virginia;[1] died 1789 in Westmoreland County, Virginia.[2]

**Thomas Smith's Parentage**: Gregory Smith and Lucy Cooke.[3]

**Life Story:** The childhood of Thomas Smith was not unlike that of other English children. Born to George Smith and Lucy Cooke of King and Queen County, Virginia in 1739,[4] he grew up in an

---

[1] Louise Pecquet du Bellet, *Some Prominent Virginia Families: Volume 4* (Lynchburg, Virginia: J. P. Bell Company, 1907) 81; digital images, *Google Books* (http://www.books.google.com: accessed 19 February 2018).

[2] Pecquet du Bellet, *Some Prominent Virginia Families: Volume 4*, 81.

[3] Ibid

[4] Pecquet du Bellet, *Some Prominent Virginia Families: Volume 4*, 81.

Anglican household. A member of the Church of England, the colony's official denomination, he was expected to show absolute loyalty to the church and the British government.

In his youth, Thomas witnessed the persecution and discrimination imposed on those who dissented from the English Church. Presbyterians, Quakers, and Baptists all suffered under the church-state government of Great Britain. The Act of Toleration of 1689, however, decreed that all dissenters had to pledge an oath of allegiance, thereby, granting religious tolerance.[5] Unfortunately, this practice was rarely observed in Virginia.

During this time, Thomas Smith's father contributed to Stratton Major Parish by processioning new land,[6] dissenters worshiped in preapproved meetinghouses. Unaware of the consequences of this liberal policy, it was not until the mid-1700s that large numbers of Anglicans converted to other denominations.

While Thomas attended church services in accordance with the practice of his parents. Recognizing the value of loyalty to the English government, he was aware that he was safe from the punishments imposed on religious dissenters. While he worshiped without duress, those who were members of other Christian doctrines suffered greatly. This became apparent to Thomas as he matured into adulthood.

Brought to court and fined for their disobedience, Baptists, Presbyterians, and Quakers also risked being jailed. As a member of the established Church, Thomas understood why there was such apprehension against them. Known for their evangelical message,

---

[5] Thomas S. Kidd, *Encyclopedia Virginia* (https://www.encyclopediavirginia.org/: accessed 26 February 2018), "Action of Toleration (1689)."

[6] Churchhill Gibson Chamberlayne, *The Vestry Book of Stratton Major Parish, King and Queen County, Virginia (1729-1783)*, (1931; reprint, Baltimore, Maryland: Genealogical Publishing Company, Inc., 1999), 34, 40, 49, 59.

and determination to worship according to their own doctrines,[7] nonconformists opposed many aspects of traditional English society.

As a child, Thomas's opinion about the treatment of religious dissenters is unknown. However, a clue can be found when he turned twelve years of age. In 1751, Gregory Smith passed away, leaving Lucy a widow who afterward *"married a Mr. Booth."*[8] According to the Smith family Bible, *"Rev. Thomas said that Booth was afraid of him, and that Booth demanded that his mother send him to England to become educated, and so get him out of the way."*[9] The reasons Mr. Booth felt threatened are not explained, but one theory is that Thomas exhibited anti-British sympathies.

As a pupil in England, Thomas's new environment supported pro-British sentiment; but, ironically, it influenced him in the opposite way. While support for dissenters in Virginia became more prevalent, the opposite was true in England. Although the relationship between the colonies and Great Britain continued to remain civil, Thomas knew he would eventually have to choose a side.

Since its beginning at Jamestown in 1607, Thomas believed Virginia to be a special place. With little oversight from London, Virginia *"had an assembly to make laws and raise law taxes, and each one had its own militia."*[10] The House of Burgesses, the legislative body in Virginia, was an independent body and resisted outside interference in Virginia's government.

---

[7] J. P. Bell, Our *Quaker Friends of ye Olden Time* (1905; reprint, Bowie, Maryland: Heritage Books, Inc., 1997), 145, 247.
[8] Lyon Gardiner Tyler, Richard Lee Morton, *William and Mary Quarterly: Volume 4* (Williamsburg, Virginia: William and Mary College, 1896), 102; digital images, *Google Books* (http://www.books.google.com: accessed 13 May 2018).
[9] Gardiner, Morton, *William and Mary Quarterly: Volume 4*, 102.
[10] Nick Bunker, *An Empire on the Edge: How Britain came to Fight America* (New York, New York: Alfred A. Knopf, 2014), 26; digital images, *Google Books* (http://www.books.google.com: accessed 14 May 2018).

Originally, a private enterprise,[11] Virginia was not owned by the British government. Instead, the *"Monarchy relied on private citizens to take on the risks of settlements of discovery."*[12] It wasn't until 1624 that Virginia became a royal colony due to its inability to govern itself.

At the time Thomas began his education in England, Virginia had already lost its independence. Studying subjects important to the upper class, he learned Latin, Greek, Hebrew, writing, and polite behavior.[13] The purpose of which was to mold young men into scholars to prepare them for governmental and ecclesiastical careers.

Destined to become rector for Cople Parish in Westmoreland County, Virginia, Thomas's main focus was Latin and Greek. With the goal of transforming students into *"orators and poets,"*[14] these studies were part of the required curriculum.

Visualizing Thomas participating in Latin class can provide us a key to better understanding his upbringing. Seated in his uncomfortable, non-padded, wooden desk, he starred out the window at the rolling, mist-covered hills. As the teacher droned on about the importance of *"Ovid and Virgil"* Thomas' memories

---

[11] Nick Bunker, *An Empire on the Edge: How Britain came to Fight America* (New York, New York: Alfred A. Knopf, 2014), 24; digital images, *Google Books* (http://www.books.google.com: accessed 16 May 2018).

[12] Bunker, *An Empire on the Edge: How Britain came to Fight America*, 24.

[13] Anthony Fletcher, *Growing up in England: The Experience of Childhood, 1600-1914* (New Haven, Connecticut: Yale University Press, 2008), 5; digital images, *Google Books* (http://www.books.google.com: accessed 16 May 2018); Martin Lowther Clarke, *Classical Education In Britain: 1500-1900* (Cambridge, England: Cambridge University Press, 1959), 34; digital images, *Google Books* (http://www.books.google.com: accessed 17 May 2018).

[14] Martin Lowther Clarke, *Classical Education In Britain: 1500-1900* (Cambridge, England: Cambridge University Press, 1959), 39; digital images, *Google Books* (http://www.books.google.com: accessed 17 May 2018).

drifted back to his mother in Virginia when a paddle smacked against his desk.[15]

"Mr. Smith, this is class, pay attention. Now, would you please turn to page seven and begin reciting line one."

Quickly, flipping through his leather-bound book to the assigned page, he began reading Virgil. Around him, the other pupils repeated after Thomas as the headmaster smiled. The echo of voices filled the room as Thomas continued to work on his pronunciation.

Isolated from the discontent stirring in the colonies, Thomas also harbored mixed emotions during this time. He understood why Americans resented the British, but yet, he recognized why the English mistrusted the colonies. This personal conflict intensified over the years as clashes between the colonists and the British Empire became common occurrences.

By 1754, the ill-will between Virginia and Great Britain had reached a new threshold. The antipathy which up until then occurred occasionally was now commonplace. Tension between the French and English was deteriorating, and the threat of war was now imminent. Appointed as Britain's unofficial *"viceroy in North America,"*[16] Edward Braddock was granted unusual powers that violated the rights of the colonists. In charge of an imperial army, he was tasked with protecting the Crown's properties in the northern colonies. However, it was his second agenda that outraged men like Thomas Smith: Commanded to unify all the colonies, Braddock trampled upon the liberties of natural born English men.

---

[15] Martin Lowther Clarke, *Classical Education In Britain: 1500-*1900 (Cambridge, England: Cambridge University Press, 1959), 40; digital images, *Google Books* (http://www.books.google.com: accessed 17 May 2018).
[16] Fred Anderson, *The War That Made America* (London, England: Penguin Books, 2006), 57.

Thomas was accustomed to hearing his fellow Virginians grumble about Edward Braddock's efforts to make America like Ireland. Like Virginia, Ireland had a legislative body, but any law passed by the Irish assembly had to reflect the interests of Westminster, England.[17] As a student in Great Britain, Thomas was in an awkward position. Surrounded by loyalists, he held on to his childhood memories and patriotic ideals. But he also understood what was happening at home in Virginia.

When the French and Indian War broke out in 1754, the House of Burgesses lost the authority to manage the colony. Now overseen by General Braddock, he had the authority to command the colonial assemblies to raise soldiers and taxes.[18]

Known as the Seven Years' War, this conflict was a global event affecting the finances of Great Britain, and causing the entire country to suffer. By 1764, the English government had incurred a national debt of more than 130 million pounds.[19] Even though the British won, the economy of Virginia was in shambles.

By the end of the war, taxes imposed by the Crown were "*9 percent of the nation's income.*"[20] While farmers struggled to support their families, the government levied taxes on beer, wine, and gin.[21] From the viewpoint of the British authorities, the provinces were an untapped source of income despite the protests of the hard-pressed colonists.

---

[17] Nick Bunker, *An Empire on the Edge: How Britain came to Fight America* (New York, New York: Alfred A. Knopf, 2014), 31; digital images, *Google Books* (http://www.books.google.com: accessed 21 May 2018).
[18] Anderson, *The War That Made America*, 57.
[19] Nick Bunker, *An Empire on the Edge: How Britain came to Fight America* (New York, New York: Alfred A. Knopf, 2014), 29; digital images, *Google Books* (http://www.books.google.com: accessed 21 May 2018).
[20] Bunker, *An Empire on the Edge: How Britain came to Fight America*, 29.
[21] Ibid

On his return to Virginia in 1765, Thomas was appointed rector at Cople Parish in Westmoreland County, Virginia.[22] As a representative of the Church of England, he was charged with upholding English law; however, Thomas had no intention of being blindly obedient.

Upon his arrival to Westmoreland County, a new tax, the Stamp Act, had become a controversial issue. Under the leadership of George Grenville, Prime Minister of Great Britain, it was designed to recover the costs of the French and Indian War. Despite this seemingly harmless intention, the Stamp Act was the beginning of the end of British control in the New World. A direct tax *"on all papers used for legal documents, liquor licenses, academic degrees, newspapers, pamphlets and almanacs,"*[23] the colonists were not represented in Parliament when the tax was passed in 1765.

Thomas Smith's position as a leader was well-respected, and not only because he was the Rector. When Thomas Ludwell Lee hosted a meeting at LeedsTown in 1766 for Patriots, Thomas willingly joined. Like his countrymen that toasted "[to]*the sons of American and [to the]singing songs of liberty,*"[24] he rejected the Stamp Act and those that aligned themselves with it.
As a pastor, Thomas preached to General George Washington on May 22, 1768, at Nomini Church, and became friends with Richard Henry Lee, a famous American statesman.[25] The sermons

---

[22] Bertha Lawrence Newton Davison, *The Life of Cople Parish 1664-1964 in Westmoreland County, Virginia* (Westminster, Maryland: Heritage Books 2008), 5018.
[23] Davison, *The Life of Cople Parish 1664-1964 in Westmoreland County, Virginia*, 5018.
[24] Bertha Lawrence Newton Davison, *The Life of Cople Parish 1664-1964 in Westmoreland County, Virginia* (Westminster, Maryland: Heritage Books 2008), 5022.
[25] Bertha Lawrence Newton Davison, *The Life of Cople Parish 1664-1964 in Westmoreland County, Virginia* (Westminster, Maryland: Heritage Books 2008), 5019-5020.

he preached in his *"black Scholastic gown"*, scorned the Crown for its inability to govern.[26] Unafraid, he fundamentally changed the nature of Cople Parish, both ecclesiastically and politically.

Although not listed as a signer of the Leedstown Resolves, there is no doubt that Thomas Smith believed in the *"Constitutional rights"* of Englishmen."[27] While he declared his allegiance to King George the Third, he also believed that the British Empire had far surpassed its authority. He truly supported the idea that *"If any attempt shall be made on the liberty or property [of Englishmen]"* there should be consequences.[28]

The persistence of Thomas Smith in denouncing Parliament had a profound and lasting impact. As an influential leader in his community, he helped establish anti-British sentiment in Westmoreland County. Inspiring men to sign the Leedstown Resolves, he helped pave the way for the Declaration of Independence.

In March 1766, the Stamp Act was repealed, but another devastating law, the Declaratory Act, was passed. Insisting *"that Parliament remained sovereign in every corner of North America,"*[29] this was another insult to Thomas Smith.

And the situation would only become worse. On November 20, 1767, the Townshend Act was passed, which taxed a variety of commodities. Paint, paper, lead, glass, and tea imported from

---

[26] Bertha Lawrence Newton Davison, *The Life of Cople Parish 1664-1964 in Westmoreland County, Virginia*, 5020.

[27] Resolutions, 1766 February 27, [Leedstown, Westmoreland County, Va.], against the enforcement of the Stamp Act in Virginia; Virginia Historical Society, Richmond, Virginia.

[28] "Resolutions, 1766 February 27, [Leedstown, Westmoreland County, Va.], against the enforcement of the Stamp Act in Virginia."

[29] Nick Bunker, *An Empire on the Edge: How Britain came to Fight America* (New York, New York: Alfred A. Knopf, 2014), 34; digital images, *Google Books* (http://www.books.google.com: accessed 24 May 2018).

England were all subject to this levy.[30] Civil unrest followed in Boston, forcing the government to send in an army. This discontent, however, did not last long, and the Townshend Act was soon abolished to preserve the peace.

By 1773, the Tea Act was passed, taxing tea being imported from British East India Company.[31] Despite a lack of representation in Parliament for Virginians, this tax required all Virginians to help support the now declining company.

When Thomas Smith heard about this, Westmoreland County already was supporting the patriotic cause. However, it was not until the Boston Tea Party of 1773 that the resistance in Virginia became energized. After the Sons of Liberty dumped 342 chests of tea into the Boston Harbor, Thomas' responsibilities as a nonconformist intensified.

On June 22, 1774, Thomas and other freeholders assembled in Westmoreland County, Virginia, in defiance of the Crown.[32] Disturbed by the laws that taxed them without representation, Thomas was now part of a Committee of Safety. With the House of Burgesses having been dissolved since May 1774,[33] this was an opportunity to establish a new government.

After being *"unanimously chosen Moderator,"*[34] Thomas had the authority to largely determine the political and economic future of Westmoreland County. Using his position as a respected rector within Cople Parish, he supported the right to be *"taxed solely in*

---

[30] Danby Pickering, *The Avalon Project: Documents in Law, History, and Diplomacy* (http://avalon.law.yale.edu/18th_century/townsend_act_1767.asp: accessed 24 May 2018), "The Townsend Act."
[31] Richard Barksdale Harwell, *The Committees of Safety of Westmoreland and Fincastle* (Richmond, Virginia:Virginia State Library, 1956), 27.
[32] Matthew S. Gottlieb, *Encyclopedia Virginia* (https://www.encyclopediavirginia.org/: accessed 11 October 2018), *"House of Burgesses."*
[33] Harwell, *The Committees of Safety of Westmoreland and Fincastle*, 27.
[34] Ibid

*our provincial Assembles by Representatives feely chosen by the People."*[35] Joining Massachusetts's sentiments, he declared that taxes forced on them was an *"Attack on the Liberty and Property of British America."*[36]

Thomas and the committee also endorsed a *"non-Importing and non-exporting Plan"*[37] that prohibited trade between America and Great Britain. Responsible for encouraging economic growth, *"Tobacco, Corn, Wheat, or any Thing else"*[38] could only be sold within the colonies. They even discouraged the use of tea, a staple import of the United Kingdom.

As committed as Thomas Smith was in passing legislation, he was equally committed to seeing legislation enforced. Using his influence, he regarded *"every Man as infamous"*[39] that broke these regulations. Although he was well-respected as a rector, his role on the Committee of Safety required him to investigate cases where the law was broken.

Prior to Thomas Smith, Cople Parish had faithfully followed the ideologies and practices of the Church of England. However, by 1774, the ecclesiastical community of Westmoreland under the leadership of Thomas became active in anti-British activities.

On November 8, 1774, Thomas was involved in a hearing involving Cople Parish.[40] Although a man of compassion, he also could be ruthless in politics. As part of the Committee of Safety, he and his colleagues were tasked with deciding the fate of David

---

[35] Richard Barksdale Harwell, *The Committees of Safety of Westmoreland and Fincastle* (Richmond, Virginia:Virginia State Library, 1956), 28.

[36] Richard Barksdale Harwell, *The Committees of Safety of Westmoreland and Fincastle* (Richmond, Virginia:Virginia State Library, 1956), 29-30.

[37] Richard Barksdale Harwell, *The Committees of Safety of Westmoreland and Fincastle* (Richmond, Virginia:Virginia State Library, 1956), 29.

[38] Richard Barksdale Harwell, *The Committees of Safety of Westmoreland and Fincastle* (Richmond, Virginia:Virginia State Library, 1956), 32.

[39] Harwell, *The Committees of Safety of Westmoreland and Fincastle*, 32.

[40] Harwell, *The Committees of Safety of Westmoreland and Fincastle*, 40.

Wardrobe, a Tory. Claiming that David had published a letter that was *"false, scandalous, and inimical to America,"*[41] they prosecuted him.

Forbidding him from using the vestry house as a school, they damaged David's reputation and his career. The children that attended his classes were taken away, and he was *"regarded as a wicked enemy to America, and to be treated as such."*[42] Ordered to publish a letter of apology *"in the gazettes,"*[43] he was expected to be remorseful *"for having traduced the people here."*[44]

The following year, Thomas Smith is documented as publishing resolutions for political purposes. After Governor Dunmore stole gunpowder from Williamsburg, Virginia, on April 21, 1775, he and the committee released a series of announcements. Accusing the governor of attempting to *"enslave"* them,[45] they rebutted his claim that *"the real grievances of the colony can be only obtained by loyal and constitutional applications."*[46]

Declaring their intention *"[to]the risk of our lives [the patriots] and fortunes,"*[47] they vowed to defend the Continental Congress. With the House of Burgesses now dissolved, Thomas and his allies condemned attacks against their new legislative government. These publications encouraged the Patriots while condemning the Loyalist cause.

---

[41] Richard Barksdale Harwell, *The Committees of Safety of Westmoreland and Fincastle* (Richmond, Virginia:Virginia State Library, 1956), 33.
[42] Harwell, *The Committees of Safety of Westmoreland and Fincastle*, 33.
[43] Richard Barksdale Harwell, *The Committees of Safety of Westmoreland and Fincastle* (Richmond, Virginia:Virginia State Library, 1956), 40.
[44] Harwell, *The Committees of Safety of Westmoreland and Fincastle*, 40.
[45] Ibid
[46] Bertha Lawrence Newton Davison, *The Life of Cople Parish 1664-1964 in Westmoreland County, Virginia* (Westminster, Maryland: Heritage Books 2008), 5026.
[47] General Assembly, *Vagenweb* (http://vagenweb.org: accessed 18 October 2018), "Laws of Virginia, May 1779-3$^d$ of COMMONWEALTH."

As an anti-British activist, Thomas Smith was accustomed to being threatened. His granddaughter recalled one memorable event that occurred during the War for Independence. Warned that the British were sailing up the Potomac River, *"The family and servants fled into the house."*[48] Thomas eventually learned that it was a false alarm.

But threats to his family were not the only consequences that Thomas experienced during the American Revolution. The Church of England also had declined. On May 3, 1779, the Virginia General Assembly passed a law that suspended *"the payment of the salaries heretofore given the Clergy of the Church of England."*[49] Once boastful of their position and social status, rectors and their parishes suffered greatly under this law. As a Patriot, Thomas was pleased to witness the collapse of the British establishment, but he also suffered financial hardships because of it.

Since the start of the war, dissenters from the Church of England had begun to gain power and influence. With the break from Great Britain almost complete, they grew bolder in dismissing the Anglican Church. Although religious freedom was not yet granted, dissenters now were exempt from paying the required parish tithes.[50] With rectors and parishes no longer able to maintain themselves, the decline of the Church of England accelerated.

With financial support from the state abolished, Cople Parish was now governed by the General Assembly. With congregations now

---

[48] General Assembly, *Vagenweb,* "Laws of Virginia, May 1779-3$^d$ of COMMONWEALTH."

[49] Thomas E. Buckley, *Establishing Religious Freedom: Jefferson's Statute in Virginia* (Charlottesville, Virginia: University of Virginia Press, 2013), digital images, *Google Books* (http://www.books.google.com: accessed 18 October 2018).

[50] Bertha Lawrence Newton Davison, *The Life of Cople Parish 1664-1964 in Westmoreland County, Virginia* (Westminster, Maryland: Heritage Books 2008), 5027.

legally tied to the new government, it was not uncommon for the authority of Anglican parishes to weaken. Thomas Smith observed how other rectors still loyal to England had resigned, left for Europe or retired.[51] With America now free, many of these pastors felt conflicted over their place in society. In some cases, rectors even changed careers.

For the Rev. Thomas Smith the situation was not as bleak. Already governed by the American government, Cople Parish was receiving contributions from patriotic Anglicans and religious dissenters. While other rectors now maintained their livelihood from farming and teaching,[52] Thomas had the support of his community. As an Anglican, he was concerned about the downfall of his denomination. But as a Patriot, he saw potential in rebuilding the church in the image of American values. Another dynamic at play was that Thomas also had to deal with the failing Virginia economy. With the inflation of the Continental currency, lack of necessities, and increased taxes,[53] Cople Parish faced difficult times. Unable to import foreign products and export tobacco, the cash crop of Virginia, parish members were forced to make *"their own clothing,"*[54]

When the war ended in 1783, the country celebrated its newly-founded freedom. This victory, however, came at a substantial

---

[51] Margaret Ellen Newell, *From Dependency to Independence: Economic Revolution in Colonial New England* (London: Cornell University Press, 1998), 310; digital images, *Google Books* (http://www.books.google.com: accessed 18 October 2018).

[52] Davison, *The Life of Cople Parish 1664-1964 in Westmoreland County, Virginia*, 5027.

[53] Virginia Library Board, *Annual Report of the Library Board of the Virginia State Library, Volume 6-7* (Richmond: Virginia State Library, 1909), 143; digital images, *Google Books* (http://www.books.google.com: accessed 19 October 2018).

[54] William Stevens Perry, *A Handbook of the General Convention of the Protestant Episcopal Church, Give its History and Constitution, 1785-1877* (New York: Bible House, 1877), 10; digital images, *Google Books* (http://www.books.google.com: accessed 19 October 2018).

cost. The political and ecclesiastical controversies had left American society divided. With the new United States government now in control, the organizations that once were the pride of Great Britain were changing. These transformations also fundamentally altered the Church of England.

In order to rebuild the Anglican Church in Virginia, the General Assembly in 1784 restructured the denomination. Under the direction of the legislative body of Virginia, it was renamed the Protestant Episcopal Church. No longer associated with Great Britain, the church functioned as a separate organization. However, these circumstances were controversial. Sponsored by the United States government, the Episcopal Church was given land once owned by the Church of England.[55] Although it strengthened the Protestant Episcopal Church, it angered religious dissenters.

On October 3, 1785, while other denominations were petitioning the General Assembly to revoke this ruling, Thomas was helping to establish the Protestant Episcopal Church. Meeting in Philadelphia, Pennsylvania at the first General Convention of the Protestant Episcopal Church, he was part of a historic meeting.[56]

Although not recorded as one of the primary representatives, he witnessed and agreed with the adaptation of new policies. Pledging his allegiance to the United States, he helped alter the *"Common Book of Prayer and Administration of the Sacraments and other Rites of Ceremonies"* to reflect this update.[57] Based on

---

[55] William Stevens Perry, *A Handbook of the General Convention of the Protestant Episcopal Church, Give its History and Constitution, 1785-1877* (New York: Bible House, 1877), 15; digital images, *Google Books* (http://www.books.google.com: accessed 19 October 2018).

[56] William Stevens Perry, *A Handbook of the General Convention of the Protestant Episcopal Church, Give its History and Constitution, 1785-1877*, 15.

[57] Virginia State Library, Archives Division, *Separation of Church and State in Virginia: a Study in the Development of the Revolution* (Richmond, Virginia: Virginia State Library, 1910), 128; digital images, *Google Books* (http://www.books.google.com: accessed 19 October 2018).

this revision, Thomas also supported the oath ministers had to take to be ordained. Instead of swearing allegiance to the King of England, they swore to *"believe the Holy Scriptures of the Old and New Testament to be the word of God, and to contain all things necessary to salvation ; and I do[to] solemnly engage to confirm the doctrines and worship of the Protestant Episcopal Church, as settled and determined in the Book of Common Prayer, and Administration of Sacraments, set forth by the General Convention of the Protestant Episcopal Church in these United States."*[58]

The church-state relationship set down by this Act of Incorporation in 1784 soon would be dissolved. On November 8, 1787, the United States Senate passed a bill that granted full religious freedom.[59] After receiving a seemingly-endless number of petitions from Presbyterians, Baptists, and Moravians claiming the Bill of Rights had been violated, the last remnants of the Established Church were removed.

Two years before his death in October 1789,[60] Thomas became ill. Before passing away, whatever doubts he had about the weakening of the Protestant Episcopal Church, he understood he had changed history forever.

---

[58] Davison, *The Life of Cople Parish 1664-1964 in Westmoreland County, Virginia*, 5031.
[59] Pecquet du Bellet, *Some Prominent Virginia Families: Volume 4*, 81.
[60] Gardiner, Morton, *William and Mary Quarterly: Volume 4*, 102.

## Conclusion

The struggle for religious freedom in eighteenth-century Virginia has always been a topic of scholarly interest. Because of famous statesmen like Thomas Jefferson, freedom of religion eventually was established. However, one must not forget the less well-known patriots and their impact upon this development

The life of Thomas Smith, a rector of the Church of England, In Westmoreland County, Virginia is such an example. In a time of religious and political persecution, he grew up in a typical Anglican household. Later becoming a leading supporter of the patriotic cause, he transformed Cople Parish into a community that reinforced the Patriot cause. As a member of the Westmoreland County, Virginia, Committee of Safety, he regulated the economic, judicial, and political policies for his county, forever changing history.

As dependence on Great Britain disappeared after the American Revolution, the Church of England was dramatically altered. Renamed the Protestant Episcopal Church by the General Assembly in 1784, Thomas denomination was weakened. Once financed by the British government, the church-state relationship between the Church of England and the government would eventually dissolve.

Before his passing in 1789, Thomas Smith was harboring mixed emotions. Rejoicing in the establishment of the United States, he mourned the decline of the Protestant Episcopal Church. However, without his dedication to the Patriot cause, the history of Virginia would have been very different.

- Born to Gregory Smith and Lucy Cooke of King and Queen County, Virginia, in 1739,[61] he was raised in an Anglican household.
- A witness to the persecution and discrimination imposed on religious dissenters, he was aware that he was safe. As an Anglican, he regularly attended Church of England worship services. However, those who refused were taxed, brought to court, or jailed.
- When Gregory Smith passed in 1751, Lucy Smith married a Mr. Booth.[62] When Mr. Booth became *"afraid"* of his son-in-law, Thomas was sent to England to get him out of the way.[63]
- Receiving an education in England, he became accustomed to studying subjects important to the upper class. Learning Latin, Greek, Hebrew, writing, and polite behavior,[64] he was destined to be a leader.
- Appointed rector at Cople Parish in f, Virginia, in 1765,[65] he was charged with upholding English law. However, Thomas Smith had no intention of being obedient.
- A supporter of the Leedstown Resolves, he believed the *"Constitutional rights"* of Englishmen" were being violated.[66]
- Being *"unanimously chosen Moderator"* for the Westmoreland County, Virginia, Committee of

---

[61] Ibid
[62] Fletcher, *Growing up in England: The Experience of Childhood, 1600-1914*, 5.
[63] Davison, *The Life of Cople Parish 1664-1964 in Westmoreland County, Virginia*, 5018.
[64] Resolutions, 1766 February 27, [Leedstown, Westmoreland County, Va.], against the enforcement of the Stamp Act in Virginia."
[65] Harwell, *The Committees of Safety of Westmoreland and Fincastle*, 27.
[66] Harwell, *The Committees of Safety of Westmoreland and Fincastle*, 29-30, 40.

Safety,[67] he implemented economic, political, and judicial policies that favored the patriots.[68]
- After the General Assembly restructured the Anglican Church in 1784, it was renamed the Protestant Episcopal Church. However, these circumstances were controversial. Sponsored by the United States government, the Episcopal Church was given land once owned by the Church of England.[69]
- Attending the first General Convention of the Protestant Episcopal Church on October 3, 1785,[70] he witnessed the adaption of new policies that reinforced loyalty to the United States.[71]
- On November 8, 1787, the United States Senate passed a bill that established full religious freedom.[72] Two years later in October 1789, Thomas Smith passed away.

---

[67] Virginia Library Board, *Annual Report of the Library Board of the Virginia State Library, Volume 6-7*, 143.

[68] Perry, *A Handbook of the General Convention of the Protestant Episcopal Church, Give its History and Constitution, 1785-1877*, 10.

[69] Perry, *A Handbook of the General Convention of the Protestant Episcopal Church, Give its History and Constitution, 1785-1877*, 15.

[70] Library, Archives Division, *Separation of Church and State in Virginia: a Study in the Development of the Revolution*, 128.

[71] Davison, *The Life of Cople Parish 1664-1964 in Westmoreland County, Virginia*, 5031.

[72] Davison, *The Life of Cople Parish 1664-1964 in Westmoreland County, Virginia*, 5031.

# Index

----, Magdalen - 9

----, Peggy - 27

Act of Toleration of 1689 - 20, 58, 77, 88,

Allen, Elizabeth - 29

American Revolution - 43, 51, 56, 56, 58, 61, 65, 72, 79, 83, 85, 98, 100,

Amherst County, Virginia - 72, 79, 80, 83, 85

Asbury, Rev. Francis - 64

Austin, Richard III - 21, 27r,

Austin, Sarah - 16, 21, 23, 26

Baptist Church - 43, 44, 45, 53, 76, 88

Barham, Newsome - 31

Barrow, Abraham - 49

Barrow, Amy Lee - 50

Barrow, David - 38, 39, 40, 41, 42, 43, 44, 45, 46, 47, 48, 49, 50, 51, 52, 53, 54,55

Barrow, David Gilliam - 49

Barrow Elizabeth - 48

Barrow, Rev. Gilliam - 50

Barrow, Hinchea Gilliam - 50

Barrow Jerusha - 49

Barrow, Jonathan - 49

Barrow, Mary - 49

Barrow, Nathaniel - 48

Barrow, Sarah - 49

Barrow, William - 38, 39,

Barrow, William B - 50

Blaikley, Mary - 15, 33

Boston Tea Party - 93

Bondurant, Frances - 10,

Bonsergent Mathieu - 8

Booth, Mr. - 87, 101

Booth, Lucy - 87, 101

Bowyer, Luke - 83

Bowyer, Mary - 83

Braddock, Edward – 91 92

Brunswick County, Virginia - 38, 39, 48, 51, 52

Bryson, John - 30

Buckingham County, Virginia - 10

104

Campbell, Elizabeth – 81f

Campbell, William - 82

Christian, Anne Henry - 81

Christian, William - 81

Church of England - 4, 6, 11, 12, 17, 19, 21, 38, 39, 40, 51, 56, 56, 57, 58, 59, 60, 61, 62, 65, 66, 67, 68, 72, 75, 76, 77, 78, 83, 85, 86, 88, 91, 96, 98, 100, 101

Clark, Judith - 48

Coke, Rev. Thomas - - 60, 64

Cooke, Lucy - 87, 103

Committee of Safety – 59, 68, 93, 94, 96, 97, 100, 101,

Cople Parish - 89, 90, 91, 92, 93, 94, 95, 96, 97, 98, 99, 100, 101, 102, 103, 104

Cornwall Parish - 26, 35

Cub Creek, Virginia - 15, 21, 23, 34, 36

Cumberland County, Virginia - - 10,

Dabney, Mary - 73

Dandridge, Dorothea Spotswood - 81

Davies, Rev. Samuel - 22, 23, 40, 76, 77, 83, 85

Dickins, John - 56, 57, 58, 59, 60, 61, 62, 63, 64, 65, 66, 67, 68, 69, 70

Demuyn, Governor - 2

Dunmore, Governor - 95

England - 1, 3, 4, 10, 11, 17, 32, 55, 56, 57, 58, 65, 66, 68, 87, 88, 90, 93, 97, 101,

Foster, Nancy C - 48

Fletcher, Lucy - 49

Foster, Nancy C. - 50

Fredericksville Parish - - 34

Gibson, John - 31

Gilliam, Sarah - 38, 42, 47, 52

Goochland County, Virginia - 9

Gordon, Samuel - 21

Grenville, George - 93

Guilford County, North Carolina - 16, 26, 35,

Halifax County, North Carolina - 55

Hamilton, Jane - 16, 24,

Hamilton, Sarah - 29

Hanover County, Virginia - 20, 22, 34, 73, 74, 76, 78, 84

Henrico County - 5, 9

Henry, Anne - 80

Henry, Elizabeth - 81

Henry, Jane - 80

Henry, John - 76, 77, 79, 81,84

Henry, Lucy 81

Henry, Mary 81

Henry, Patrick - 72, 77, 78, 79, 81, 83, 85f

Henry, Sarah - 83

Henry, Sarah Winston Syme - 74, 73, 74, 75, 76, 77, 78, 79, 80, 81, 81, 82, 83, 84, 85

Henry, Susannah Madison - 82

Henry, William - 79, 81

Hicks, Francis - 29

Hicks, James - 29

Huguenots - 1, 2, 3, 4, 6, 7, 8, 10, 11, 12

Hulse, Richard - 49

Hulse, Sarah - 48

Indiana - 47, 48

Ireland - 1, 15, 16, 17, 18, 19, 20, 22, 26, 31, 32, 58, 90

Isle of Wight County, Virginia - 42, 47, 48, 51

Jefferson, Thomas - 46, 52, 102

Joyce, Andrew - 26, 30

Joyce, Alexander - 15, 16, 17, 18, 19, 20, 21, 22, 23, 24, 25, 26, 27, 28, 30, 33, 34, 35, 36

Joyce, Elisha - 26, 27, 29

Joyce Elijah - 25

Joyce, Elizabeth - 25, 31

Joyce, Esther - 24, 25, 30

Joyce, James - 25, 28

Joyce, John (Possum) - 25, 27

Joyce, Margaret - 26, 31

Joyce, Mary - 26, 31

Joyce, Robert - 26, 30

Joyce, Sarah - 25, 29

Joyce, Thomas - 15, 17, 25, 27, 32

Kentucky - 37, 38, 44, 45, 46, 47, 48, 49, 50, 52, 53, 81

King, Elizabeth - 30

King and Queen County, Virginia - 87, 86, 103

King William Parish - 5, 6, 8, 12,

Lee, Amey - 37

Lee, Richard Henry - 93

Lee, Thomas Ludwell - 91

Leedstown Resolves - 93, 94 101

Lidderdale, John - 21

Lindsay, Elizabeth - 30

Louisa County, Virginia - 19, 28, 31, 32

Lunenburg County, Virginia - 15, 21, 27, 28, 31, 33, 34, 35,

Mackey, Joel - 29

Madison, James – 79f

Madison, Thomas - 81

Malet, Etienne - 10

Manakin Town - 5, 6, 7, 8, 9, 10

Marshall, Ann Goodwin - 50

Meredith Jane, - 82

Meredith, Samuel - 82

Methodist Episcopal Church - 56, 61, 63, 64, 65, 66,

Martin, Maria - 2

Meriwether, Mildred - 80

McClure, Samuel - 50

Missouri - 49

Morton, John - 26

Native Americans - 19, 23, 34

New York - 4, 9, 11

Norfolk, Virginia - 5

Penn, William - 18

Pennsylvania - 18, 19, 31, 32, 33, 55, 98,

Perault, Olive - 4, 9

Philipe, Mr. - 6, 7, 12

Presbyterian Church - 2, 15, 17, 22, 31, 34, 77, 82

Presbytery of Hanover - 22, 23, 34

Prince Edward County, Virginia - 16, 25, 35,

Rockingham County, North Carolina - 26, 27, 28, 29, 30, 31

Russel, Elizabeth - 82

Russel, William - 82

Saint Paul's Parish - 21, 75s, 78, 83

Sallé, Abraham - 1, 2, 3, 4, 5, 6, 7, 8, 9, 10, 11, 12, 13

Sallé Jacob - 4, 5, 9, 12

Sallé, Jean - 2

Sallé, Isaac - 9

Sallé, Olive Magdalen - 10

Sallé, (Pierre) Peter - 10,

Sallé, William - 10,

Scholl, Rachel - 50

Shackelford, Sarah - 29

Shelton, Sarah - 81

Shepard, James - 26

Slavery – 35, 38, 41, 42, 44, 46, 47, 49, 50, 51, 52, 56, 57, 59, 61, 66, 67, 69,

Smith, Gregory - 86, 87, 89, 101

Smith, Lucy 85, 87, 101

Smith, Thomas - 86, 87, 88, 89, 90, 91, 92, 93, 94, 95, 96, 97, 98, 99, 100, 101, 102, 103, 104

Smyth County, Virginia - 81

Spaulding, Alexander - 21

Stamp Act - 94

Southampton County, Virginia - 44, 51

Stratton Major Parish - 88

Syme, John - 76, 74, 75, 79, 82, 83

Syme, John Jr. - 79

Syme, Sarah - 73, 74, 79, 82, 83

Tate, Margaret "Peggy" - 28

Tatman, Ruth - 50

Tea Act - 95

Thompson, Zachariah - 39, 40, 41, 52

Wardrobe, Thomas - 95

Washington, George - 91

Wesley, Rev. John - 58, 63, 68

Westmoreland County, Virginia - 87, 88, 91, 93, 94, 99, 103,

William III, King - 5,

Williamsburg, Virginia - 97

Winston, Isaac - 72, 73, 74, 82

Winston, Sarah - 71, 72, 73, 82,

Wood, Lucy - 81

Wood, Valentine - 82

Woodward, William - 48

Yancy, Elizabeth - 56

108